THE MASTER IN 'AKKÁ
by Myron H. Phelps

'ABDU'L-BAHÁ
The Master.

THE MASTER IN 'AKKÁ

by Myron H. Phelps

including the recollections of
The Greatest Holy Leaf

REVISED AND ANNOTATED

with a new foreword by
Marzieh Gail

KALIMÁT PRESS
LOS ANGELES

These chapters are reprinted from *Life and Teachings of
Abbas Effendi: A Study of the Religion of the Babis, or Beha'is,
Founded by the Persian Bab and by his Successors, Beha Ullah
and Abbas Effendi* by Myron H. Phelps, Second Revised
Edition, published in 1912 by G. P. Putnam's Sons,
New York and London.

Library of Congress Cataloging in Publication Data

Phelps, Myron H. (Myron Henry), 1856–1916.
The master in 'Akká.

"Reprinted from Life and teachings of Abbas Effendi."
2nd rev. ed. New York; London: Putnam, 1912.
Bibliography: p. 159
1. 'Abdu'l-Bahá, 1844–1921. I. Gail, Marzieh. II. Title.
BP393.P525 1985 297'.89'0924 85–24031
ISBN 9-933770-49-9

CONTENTS

FAMILIAR 'AKKÁ VOICES
by Marzieh Gail

LIFE AND TEACHINGS

OF

ABBAS EFFENDI

A STUDY OF THE RELIGION OF THE BABIS, OR BEHA'IS
FOUNDED BY THE PERSIAN BAB AND BY HIS SUC-
CESSORS, BEHA ULLAH AND ABBAS EFFENDI

BY

MYRON H. PHELPS
of the New York Bar

WITH AN INTRODUCTION BY

EDWARD GRANVILLE BROWNE, M.A., M.R.A.S.
Fellow of Pembroke College, Sir Thomas Adams' Professor of
Arabic and some time Lecturer in Persian in the University
of Cambridge, Author of " A Traveller's Narrative "
" The New History of Mírzá 'Alí Muhammad
the Bab," etc.

G. P. PUTNAM'S SONS
NEW YORK & LONDON
The Knickerbocker Press
1903

TITLE PAGE TO FIRST EDITION
of *Life and Teachings of Abbas Effendi* by Myron H. Phelps.

In Cairo, on March 8, 1903, Myron H. Phelps of the New York Bar finished the introduction to his *Life and Teachings of Abbas Effendi*, and signed it with his three initials.

Phelps had dedicated the work to Countess M. A. de S. Canavarro because it was she who attracted his attention "to the real character and significance of the Beha'i Movement." (His then widely used but erroneous spelling of Bahá'í was caused by the fact that Persian does not write the short vowels, and some used to read the first "a" as "e.")

He went on to say that her "clear insight" was largely responsible for "such success as I may have had in reaching a correct appreciation and understanding of the teachings of Abbas Effendi." He and the Countess had "worked together over all parts of the book," and it should have been published over their two names, "but since she does not wish this, I am obliged to content myself with stating the facts." He also said, in the rather apologetic manner favored by authors of the day, that he was aware of the book's "many deficiencies" and possibly "some errors" and asked his readers to send him corrections in care of his publishers, G. P. Putnam's Sons, New York and London.

It so happened that the publisher, G. H. Putnam, was an old friend of the orientalist, Edward Granville Browne—whom Phelps had met in Cairo, probably in the spring of 1903—and at Putnam's request Browne supplied the book with an introduction of his own, dated at Cambridge, September 27, 1903.

Browne says he read the work "with equal pleasure and satisfaction." He says "the whole book is to me full of familiar echoes of the voices to which I so eagerly listened when I visited 'Akká thirteen years ago, in the days when Bahá'u'lláh himself still dwelt amongst mankind." (p. vii)

Browne is, of course, mistaken when he says that the book is "a faithful and trustworthy exposition of the views of Abbas Effendi, 'the Master of 'Akká', and his followers." When studying the text of a proposed reprint sent in for evaluation by Kalimát Press, the Research Department of the Universal House of Justice identified forty inaccuracies during its initial review. (All are noted here in footnotes and references.) Phelps does not correctly present the Bahá'í Teachings, since, in the circumstances, exegesis was beyond him.

"I do not," he writes, "for a moment conceive that I have arrived at a full understanding of the tenets of the [Bahá'í] religion and the philosophy underlying it in all their scope and detail." He says the time was far too short for his investigation—he was there in 'Akká for one month, December 1902 — and accurate renderings into a European language were not available. (p. xli)

Indeed it would not be till the following year, 1904, that Laura Barney would begin to compile her priceless and authoritative account of 'Abdu'l-Bahá's table talks, *Some Answered Questions*. Laura, an American heiress, was an intellectual; she had language skills, being bilingual in French and English; and she studied Persian in the Holy Land. Furthermore she was helped in her task by the erudite French scholar Hippolyte Dreyfus. Their work on this book drew Laura and Hippolyte together, their marriage resulted, and as is the custom in some countries, the couple was known as the Hippolyte Dreyfus-Barneys. (Thanks to a strange twist of fate, Laura, whose memory history will cherish, is passed over by many of her contemporaries, while her sister Natalie appears in turn of the century memoirs and is the subject of several full-length biographies, including a recent one by Jean Chalon.)

In any case, Laura's book, *Some Answered Questions*, published in London, would not appear until 1908. Hippolyte brought out his French translation of the same talks, published in Paris by Leroux, and he called it *Les Leçons de Saint-Jean-d'Acre.*

Laura says that *Some Answered Questions* is "in no way complete and exhaustive." The teachings, given her between 1904 and 1906, were, she tells us, deliberately simplified by 'Abdu'l-Bahá "to correspond to my rudimentary knowledge," and they were not presented in order. Here, the Master is "the teacher adapting Himself to His pupil." He said He had given her His "tired moments." Sometimes "days and even weeks would pass" before He had time to continue with the lessons: "But I could well be patient, for I had always before me the greater lesson—the lesson of His personal life."

IT IS THIS personal life of the Master which Phelps has exceptionally well recorded in his book. For the rest, the interviews of Madame Canavarro with Khánum, 'Abdu'l-Bahá's sister, are of great interest for Khánum's memories of the tragic events she had herself lived through. Otherwise one might well be misdirected if one relied on this text for a study of the deeper teachings, and for this reason Kalimát Press has chosen to reprint only portions of the book. Phelps has certainly kept for posterity certain aspects of 'Abdu'l-Bahá's daily practice, even certain gestures, which touch the heart, and mean all the more to Bahá'ís because the Master was appointed by His Father not only as Head and Interpreter of the Faith, but as the example for all believers (each as best he can) to follow.

The fact that Phelps was not a declared Bahá'í, although undoubtedly close and sympathetic to this religion, is probably an advantage to the non-Bahá'í reader. Here is an educated man, attracted to this Faith but not specifically an adherent, simply writing out the best way he knew, what he had learned and witnessed. His book has the same status as all other "pilgrims' reports," subjective accounts which returned pilgrims are welcome, even encouraged to share, but which necessarily cannot be regarded as authoritative if one wishes to go seriously into the Teachings. In a religion which has no clergy but which, unlike most other religions—except Islam—does possess its authoritative, original Texts, obviously one bases belief on these Texts rather than on the impressions of this or the other reporter. (Bahá'ís are directed by Bahá'u'lláh to "look into all things with a searching eye," [*Tablets*, p. 157]; they may well, throughout life, from their ongoing studies and contacts with other students of the Faith, alter or develop their own understanding of this or that teaching, but are always aware that their personal interpretation has no authority over anyone else. In trying to attract the attention of the world to the Faith of Bahá'u'lláh, Bahá'ís inevitably return again and again to their authorized Texts.)

Religion in his time was, thought Myron Phelps, "almost throughout the world . . . stagnant and faith is dead." But there in the Holy Land he found "a demonstration that it is capable of revival. Such a spectacle as the ideal, Christlike life of Abbas Effendi has in it an immense probative and stimulating power. "As a result of reflections of this kind" he tells us, "came the impulse to prepare this book."

And so for a month he witnessed, and spoke with

xiii

'ABDU'L-BAHÁ NEAR THE SHRINE OF THE BÁB
with a group of Bahá'ís. Note Shoghi Effendi, far left, and Western Bahá'ís
directly behind the Master.

family members and others who had long witnessed, the Master's way of being. Bahá'ís learn from childhood that only this kind of being can win them their goal—the spiritual conquest of the planet. The Guardian, Shoghi Effendi, has written that not by noble principles, not by the force of numbers, not even by staunch faith and great enthusiasm, can Bahá'ís vindicate "the supreme claim of the Abhá Revelation. One thing and only one thing will unfailingly and alone secure the undoubted triumph of this sacred Cause, namely, the extent to which our own inner life and private character mirror forth . . . the splendor of those eternal principles proclaimed by Bahá'u'lláh." (*Bahá'í Administration*, p. 57)

There is no arguing with a life such as the Master led, and He lived under close scrutiny. During forty years of His time on earth, He was a prisoner, and watched. Always there were people about Him, disciples, guests, notables, inquirers. What He was drew them—not only the half-wild poor, living in their hovels and out on the desert, but leading individuals from East and West—to the narrow, sandy stretch along the Mediterranean where He passed most of His days. It was a fact which His enemies, especially those members of His Household who broke with Him, could never forgive. Why had Bahá'u'lláh singled Him out and called Him "the Master"? Why did strangers come to Him from unknown America and offer Him lifelong devotion? Why not to them instead? Why would a Persian prince become His follower? Why would the learned take notes when He spoke?

One thinks back to the time of Bahá'u'lláh, who also attracted murderous hostility, though He was also "the object of a devotion and love," wrote E. G. Browne, "which kings might envy." One reads, for example, that although He came as a prisoner and exile, He was greeted with great homage the day He entered Constantinople. That day His hostile half brother, Mírzá Yaḥyá, running along "by his own choice, behind Bahá'u'lláh's carriage," was heard by the chronicler Nabíl to tell his evil genius, Siyyid Muḥammad: "Had I not chosen to hide myself, had I revealed my identity, the honor accorded Him (Bahá'u'lláh) on this day would have been mine too." (*God Passes By*, p. 155) Helpless rage at another's perfection can lead to murder of the innocent. Joseph, down the ages, is time and again thrown into the well.

SIDELIGHTS on how this book was written are found in the *Khátirát-i Nuh Sálih* of Dr. Yúnis Khán, his *Nine Years of Memories* of the days when he lived in the Holy Land.

He tells how, very gradually, a few Westerners who implored to come received permission, in spite of the Master's precarious situation, and appeared discreetly, singly or in small groups. Among the early ones were two Americans, Madame de Canavarro and her brother

xvi

DR. YÚNIS KHAN AFRÚKHTIH
Author of *Khátirát-i Nuh Sálih (Nine Years of Memories)*.

in Buddhism, Myron Phelps. Fortunately by then, the town residence of Bahá'u'lláh had been vacated and was in the Master's hands, so the two were accommodated there.

Madame de Canavarro had been an ardent Buddhist, was a teacher of that Faith, and had expended large sums over many years to promote her beliefs. She had sacrificed her substance for the work, and was widely known for it. She belonged to a leading family, was thoroughly conversant with the new philosophy of the West, as well as with the Sufism of India, and she had had the Gospel of Buddha translated into English and French. Now, by way of Buddhism, she had come to the Bahá'í Faith. She was about forty-five or fifty, frail in health but joyous in spirit. Phelps, her co-religionist, accompanied her to 'Akká. He had a great talent for literary work and was making a record of his experiences.

When the Countess arrived, she humbly kissed the hand of 'Abdu'l-Bahá. He showed her great kindness, and she was received by the ladies of the Household in the *andarún*. The day following her arrival, conversations at table with the Master began. Unlike recent visitors, Mr. Breakwell and the sons of Mr. Dodge, she asked many questions and Phelps wrote down the answers. But the problem was this: The two Buddhists differed as to their ideas and beliefs, and the book which was being compiled had to be agreeable to both. For this reason the Master was put to great trouble clarifying questions for both of them.

"The lady asks a question," says Dr. Yúnis K͟hán in his account, "I translate it and then give her the Master's reply. Mr. Phelps writes it all down very rapidly—but since the questioner and the writer have opposing viewpoints it becomes exceedingly difficult to communicate the response to these two conflicting minds, and the need to repeat it all places a burden on the Master. One brief section dealing with Buddha or other Prophets presented no problems. But for the important section dealing with reincarnation, Phelps insisted in setting forth his preferences and beliefs, or would slant the material in such a way as to please the many believers in reincarnation who are in Europe— thus attracting readers and sales—and this problem obtained throughout the writing of the book.

"On the second or third day at the luncheon table, when complex matters began to be introduced, a fracas suddenly broke out and the occasion of it was this: A question which was obvious and basic in Bahá'í philosophy seemed abstruse to the lady and accordingly it was repeated a number of times until at last it was made clear. At this moment the lady turned on me, angrily attacked me and became so agitated that she could not address the problem with calm. The Master repeatedly asked me, 'What is she saying?' but the lady gave me no opportunity to grasp the subject and present it to the Master.

"After a considerable uproar, she seemed to be saying, 'You people of the East, why should you be in the forefront of religion, in view of the fact that you are not all that advanced, and why should we Westerners need to receive our ideas from you? Where did you come from, that we should need you? In the first place you do not possess such attainments that you should have the capacity to understand matters of this kind. When we have explained something to you and imparted some line of thought, then we have to wait for your answer. If it weren't for us from the West how would you grasp any of these things—and then as soon as you have grasped the matter, you understand the answer first, and then I have to understand it from you. Worst of all, you learn the secrets of Heaven and the divine truths directly from the Master (that is, you drink from the source), while we hear it only from your tongue (that is, we drink stagnant water). Why must I concentrate my eyes and ears on what comes out of your mouth, and sit waiting till I receive my answer?'

"As soon as I understood her comments I presented them to the Master. Yes, it is in such situations that His dignified manner and His loving smiles can defeat a whole world. He gazed tenderly upon her and said, 'Tell her that the influence of the secrets of Heaven is spiritual, and not of the body. Ear and tongue are material tools. Unless the spirit be ready to recieve the bounties of God, of what use are eye and ear? These spiritual themes are making an impact on your heart, I am speaking with you by the power of the Spirit, and you, with complete concentration and pure intent, and an illumined heart, are receiving the divine effulgences.

The essential is a true inner bond between us. God be praised that this firm, inward, spiritual tie is present. Whatever you have understood thus far has reached you from the breaths of the Holy Spirit, and my spiritual connection with you is immediate and direct. The tongue of the interpreter is but a material tool.'

"Following this the Master cited examples of the devotion and success of the disciples of Christ, and said that in this wondrous age as well, souls who had neither physical sight nor hearing had attained to faith and had guided others. In brief, the lady was now content and expressed her pleasure, and peace was established between the two of us. She stayed over a month and important philosophical and mystical problems were solved for her. Some of these were published by Mr. Phelps in his book, some the lady kept in her heart.

"As for the book, the first section, telling of the impressions of Phelps and the things he witnessed, is very sweet, sensitive and moving. The other section, describing the journeys of Bahá'u'lláh and the Holy Household, the exile from Tehran to Baghdad, to Constantinople and Adrianople and 'Akká, is also very accurate and well established. This section, which the lady heard from the Greatest Holy Leaf herself, the translator being one of the Master's daughters, she wrote down and gave to Mr. Phelps. As to the other part, however, many mistakes crept into it with regard to such matters as reincarnation. I translated half the book three or four times, and it was brought to the Master's attention. Again, I either translated it into English or described the material to Mr. Phelps, and the Master corrected it. Nevertheless, the main part as published was contrary to the Master's teachings. Madame de Canavarro herself would understand His teachings, but Mr. Phelps would write as he pleased. Finally the two ended their days here in good spirits and for a considerable time thereafter letters would come from Madame de Canavarro telling of her services to the Cause."

No doubt this account by Dr. Yúnis Khán explains why, as stated by Phelps in his introduction, the Countess did not wish the book to be published over their two joint names.

THROUGH Madam Canavarro, Phelps was able to obtain, as it were, interviews in absentia with Bahíyyih Khánum, "The Lady." This was 'Abdu'l-Bahá's sister, two years younger than Himself, who would in future, more than once, be in effect Regent of the Bahá'í World. She, the Greatest Holy Leaf, spoke no English, but young women in the Household, notably Rúḥá Khánum and her sister Munavvar, daughters of the Master, could serve as translators. The talks were not written down as Khánum spoke, they were recorded only after the lapse of a few hours and shared with Phelps in installments.

He explains why he could not meet Khánum in person. It was because of the restrictions of Islamic custom,

BAHÍYYIH KHÁNUM, THE GREATEST HOLY LEAF

which the Bahá'ís "carefully observe for the sake of peace and harmony." The ladies, captives in that Muslim country, wore the veil and except for close relatives did not meet with men. The present narrative from Khánum is probably the longest and most valuable of any she has left us.

Here this graceful and patrician lady, fragile, her health forever impaired by exile and imprisonment, tells the story of her Brother, whose sufferings and those of their parents she had shared from childhood. She tells how it was for them in Tehran, during the days after an attempt was made on the life of the shah, and how, until His innocence was proved, Bahá'u'lláh was chained underground with criminals in the shah's Black Pit. How the family's house was pillaged, and in one day they passed from great wealth to destitution, and her mother had to exchange the gold buttons on their clothing for food. How she, a little girl then, spent days of terror alone with her small brother in their ruined house, listening to the cries of mobs who were torturing and killing her fellow believers in the streets, expecting at every moment to hear that Bahá'u'lláh was no more. Then came their exile to Baghdad, their extreme poverty at the beginning, the plots of Bahá'u'lláh's half brother Mírzá Yaḥyá, Bahá'u'lláh's two years absence in the wilderness, His return and the growing prosperity of the Faith. How word was carried to the two Muslim rulers, the shah and the sultan, of the spread of the Teachings, and brought on their exile to Constantinople. How they were expelled from Constantinople and exiled in summer clothes and with scanty food through cold so terrible that the upper reaches of the Euphrates froze over for forty days—to five years of captivity in Adrianople. Then the final exile to the fortress town of 'Akká. Khánum said that after landing in 'Akká, they had to walk through cursing, taunting mobs to the army barracks where they were jailed. Most were ailing, and Bahá'u'lláh and herself perhaps the sickest of all. As they entered the prison, the great door was bolted behind them, they were up to their ankles in mud, and the smell of excrement was so strong that Khánum fainted away and there was no place to lay her down. A man there was weaving a mat for the soldiers, and she was placed on this mat and brought back to herself with water from a puddle on the floor, which the weaver was using for his rushes. The prisoners came down with typhoid and dysentery, but were allowed no doctor or medicine. There were seventy of them, and four died.

Then her younger brother Mihdí fell from the roof of the barracks through an unguarded skylight, to his death. And throughout all the tragedies 'Abdu'l-Bahá, whatever His own sufferings, served His Father as manager of the family and their fellow captives, as well as cook, comforter and nurse.

BROWNE SPEAKS in his introductory essay to Phelps's book of "the most remarkable triumph of the Bahá'í religion . . . the marvellous success achieved in recent years by its missionaries in the United States of America. . . . Once again in the world's history has the East vindicated her claim to teach religion to the West . . . " It was precisely when these words were being written that Mírzá Abu'l-Faḍl with Ali-Kuli Khan as his interpreter were reaching large and enthusiastic audiences in America. Browne cites a number of reasons for the Christian missionary's "almost complete failure" in Muslim countries. He points out that "Western Christianity, save in the rarest cases, is more Western than Christian, more racial than religious." Islam has nothing against racial intermarriage while "many even of the most excellent and earnest Christian missionaries . . . whom Europe and America send to Asia and Africa would be far less shocked at the idea of receiving on terms of intimacy in their house or at their table a white-skinned atheist than a dark-skinned believer."

Another reason Browne gives for Bábí-Bahá'í success in gaining adherents is that these believers accept "the divine inspiration of the Qur'án" and the prophethood of Muḥammad, and he describes the insoluble problem confronting the Christian missionary: the Qur'án teaches the validity of the religions gone before, therefore arguing the Muslims out of their Book converts them "not to Christianity but to Scepticism or Atheism."

"What indeed," he asks, "could be more illogical . . . than to devote much time and labour to the composition of controversial works which endeavour to prove,

A VIEW OF 'AKKÁ, circa 1880

EDWARD G. BROWNE
in Persian costume.

in one and the same breath, *first*, that the Qur'án is a lying imposture, and, *secondly*, that it bears witness to the truth of Christ's mission, as though any value attached to the testimony of one proved a liar!''

The Bábí or Bahá'í, however, "admits that Muhammad was the Prophet of God and that the Qur'án is the Word of God, denies nothing but their finality, and does not discredit his own witness when he draws from that source arguments to prove his faith.'' (pp. xix–xx)

Browne is obviously wrong when he says of our beliefs, "their doctrine . . . is at most a new synthesis of old ideas . . . '' Where in previous religions do we find sex equality, world language, universal education, world federation, administration of (Bahá'í) affairs through prayer and consultation by elected representatives of the "man in the street,'' and indeed the giving to that "ordinary'' man and woman an individual voice that can become effective nationally and even globally through the Bahá'í system? If, however, Browne refers to the repetition by the Báb and Bahá'u'lláh, and every other Manifestation of God, of the same, essential truths at the core of all religions (which might be summed up in George Herbert's "Love God and love your neighbor, work and pray''), here one can understand why, as Phelps quotes Him, the Master says, "Every one receiving these instructions will think, 'How like my own religion!' '' (p. 128)

Telling of the impact which their belief exerts on the conduct of these believers, the "high ethical standard inculcated'' by the Báb and Bahá'u'lláh, Browne remarks on the earnestness of followers of the new Faith, "while the great majority of Jews, Christians, and Muhammadans are what they are simply by reason of the circumstances of their birth." He lists two advantages which the Bahá'í religion enjoys over Christianity, Islam, "or any other of the older world-religions" —thus inferentially already calling the Faith a world religion: first, "its freedom from . . . lukewarm adherents . . ." and second, he thinks, that "towards other religions, especially Christianity, they [the Bahá'ís] would . . . be more tolerant than are the Muhammadans . . ." He does not hesitate to suggest that once in power, the believers as he knew them might not prove so tolerant toward native foes, but says that once dominant in Persia "they would, I am convinced, prove infinitely more progressive, and Persia as a country might not improbably gain enormously both in wealth and power by the change." (p. xxiv)

He bases this on his own visit to Persia, descibed in his classic *A Year Amongst the Persians*, when he spent twelve months (1887–88) in that country. A modern Bahá'í, reading this work, feels that Browne was most of the time with believers who were just emerging from Islam, who in many cases had not had the new teachings of Bahá'u'lláh, who indeed had much of the time been cut off from the imprisoned, then the martyred Báb, and now, since 1852, from their Leader in exile—that Leader Who "recast, expanded, and liberalized" the Báb's teachings and Whose own teachings were later "expounded, reaffirmed and amplified" by

His appointed Interpreter, the Master. (*God Passes By*, p. xvii)

Browne, the scholar, writes of Phelps inferentially *de haut en bas*, as almost a passerby. Once finished with the compliments normal in an introduction, we learn that Phelps did not know the languages (as did Browne), that Phelps had not spent a long time with the believers (as had Browne), that Phelps did not know the Persian classics (as did Browne), and Phelps "goes, perhaps, rather too far . . . "

Harking back, however, to the dawn of the Faith, Browne was caught up in unscholarly fervor, and could not help ending his remarks with the martyr's song, sung in 1852 by Sulaymán <u>Kh</u>án, the one with lighted candles burning in his wounds as, through jeering mobs, he walked and danced to his death:

> *In this hand the wine-cup, in this the*
> *Loved One's tress,*
> *So would I dance across the market place.* *

MYRON PHELPS begins his own personal introduction to this book by stating of the Bahá'í Faith: "We are here in the presence of a great force, destined to have a far-reaching influence upon the thoughts and lives of men." (p. xxvii)

"Fascinating indeed," he continues, "are those mysterious and mighty movements which . . . with a certain rhythmic sequence and regularity, have from

*Retranslated by M.G. — ED.

the earliest days swept over the earth . . . changing individual habits and social customs . . . moulding the lives of vast masses of mankind. A Confucius, a Zoroaster, a Buddha, a Christ, a Mahomet, is born as other men, lives the ordinary span of human life, and dies as others, but by his brief presence the face of the world is changed.''

Over eighty years ago, Phelps referred to the Bahá'í religion as ''a religious faith which gives promise of becoming, at no very distant time, one of the recognised great religions of the world.'' His appreciation, so early in the century when the general public knew little of the Bahá'í teachings, does him much credit. Many eminences, leaders in their various fields, did indeed pay it their tributes—this is a matter of record—but even now when our Faith is established worldwide, it takes a special type of mind to objectively consider the stupendous claim of Bahá'u'lláh, that He is the Promised One of all religions.

Browne tells how he himself was excoriated for his interest. He had been ''irresistibly attracted'' to the Báb by Count de Gobineau's landmark study, *Les Religions et les Philosophies dans l'Asie Centrale*. He traveled to Persia, and later had four interviews with Bahá'u'lláh as His guest in the mansion of Bahjí, April 15–20, 1890. It was during this visit that 'Abdu'l-Bahá handed Browne the manuscript of His (anonymously written) *A Traveller's Narrative*. Browne translated it and was savagely attacked for his pains, in the *Oxford Magazine*, May 25, 1892.

In his introduction to Phelps's book, ten years after the event, Browne quotes portions of this attack, which ended with the statement that his article prefacing the translation displayed "a personal attitude almost inconceivable in a rational European . . . " The critic also avers that "speaking candidly as a layman," he considers "the history of a recent sect which has affected the least important part of the Moslem world (nor that part very deeply) and is founded on a personal claim which will not bear investigation for a moment" is "quite unworthy of the learning and labour which the author has brought to bear upon it." And adds that "the prominence given to the 'Báb' in this book is an absurd violation of historical perspective; and the translation of the *Traveller's Narrative* a waste of the powers and opportunities of a Persian scholar." (p. xiii n)

The attention of Phelps was drawn to 'Akká because he saw in the Báb and Bahá'u'lláh and the unnumbered Persian martyrs, successors to the age-old glory that had always recurred in the past. He wished to observe the third figure, still living, of a remarkable triumvirate, two of them Messengers from God, the third now invested with the headship of the Faith. What impressed him much was the fact that Bahá'ís recognize other faiths "as equally divine in origin" with their own. And again, that the Bahá'í Faith has "a vital and effective power to mould life."

These things were a revelation to him, Phelps says. He saw in what he had witnessed there in 'Akká "the potentiality of immense good to other nations of the world by impelling a recognition of the real strength and greatness of the spirit of true religion, under whatever external form it may appear. Out of such reflections "came the impulse to prepare this book." (p. xlii)

Inevitably, students of the Bahá'í Faith will be impatient to add explanatory material to what they find here. There is Browne's note, for example, on page 42, quoting Mírzá Yaḥyá, the murderous half brother of Bahá'u'lláh, to the effect that in Adrianople Bahá'u'lláh attempted to poison *him*, not the reverse, as was the case—the brother giving Him poison which inflicted on Bahá'u'lláh a month-long illness and left Him with a tremor in His hand for the rest of His life. Again in Adrianople, as an estranged wife of the sanguinary Mírzá Yaḥyá revealed, he poisoned the Holy Family's well. It was also in that city that he tried to induce Salmání, the devoted barber of Bahá'u'lláh, who describes in *My Memories of Bahá'u'lláh* the plot to assassinate the Messenger of God in His bath.

Discussing Browne's statement in the latter's notes on *A Traveller's Narrative* (p. 371 ff.), where Browne lists accusations by the half brother and states—with the same jingoism that Browne criticizes in the Christian missionaries—that after all, "the removal of persons inimical to a religious movement by . . . religious assassination is a thing far less repugnant to the Eastern than to the Western mind." Phelps challenges the implication: "A transparent fabrication," he says of the charges, "incredible to anyone familiar with the character and teachings of the Beha'is." "I must protest most energetically against Professor Browne's suggestion that any traits of Oriental character shared by the leaders of Beha'ism be assumed as possibly closing their eyes to the iniquity of such proceedings in support of their cause . . . I wish to place on record the fact that my own acquaintance with the Beha'is and the spirit which animates them makes it inconceivable to me that such utter perversion of moral sense, however possible it may generally be to the Oriental type of character, about which I here express no opinion, could under any circumstances characterise their policy as a body or the policy of their leaders." (pp. 42, 43 n)

A caveat should be added to Phelps's reporting of the Master's words on hunting, reproduced here, and how He did not care for this sport: hunting in moderation is not forbidden to Bahá'ís, as one learns from the Aqdas, Bahá'u'lláh's Book of Laws.

Two historic selections from Browne, which Phelps includes, are the word-portrait of 'Abdu'l-Bahá as Browne saw Him in 1890, when the Master was forty-six, and the now world-famous, first interview that the orientalist was privileged to have with Bahá'u'lláh during that same visit.

THE HISTORIAN Hasan Balyuzi, in his in-depth study, *'Abdu'l-Bahá: The Centre of the Covenant of Bahá'u'lláh,* quotes extensively from the present work, and tells how Phelps describes his visit to 'Akká as one of the most memorable months of his life, "for not only was I able to gain a satisfactory general view of this religion, but I made the acquaintance of Abbas Effendi, who is easily the most remarkable man whom it has ever been my fortune to meet." (p. 97)

In their review of *The Life and Teachings of Abbas Effendi*, Kazem and Firuz Kazemzadeh pointed out that even then, fifty years after 'Abdu'l-Bahá's passing, there was no adequate biography of the Master (this was before Mr. Balyuzi's book was available, 1971). Necessary documents were not at hand, sources were in archives on at least three continents, language barriers including Persian and Arabic narrowed the number of researchers. At that time the authors listed only five biographers: Phelps, H. C. Ives, M. Zarqání, Dr. H. Mu'ayyad, and Dr. Yúnis Khán Afrúkhtih. The present book by Phelps was "the first attempt to write a full-length study of 'Abdu'l-Bahá in English."

Phelps did not have the necessary historical background—this was long before the Guardian's translation of Nabíl's chronicle, *The Dawn-Breakers*, and the writing of his own master work, *God Passes By*. These reviewers feel that the pages of narrative from the Greatest Holy Leaf are the "marrow" of this book, but state that as a guide to Bahá'í beliefs Phelps cannot be relied on. They explain that the Bahá'í Faith "does not synthesize" but "unifies and fulfills the great religions of the past," and that "the very basis on which . . . its acceptance of other religions rests—the concepts of progressive revelation and of the relativity of religious truth—is strikingly novel." (*World Order Magazine,* Fall, 1971)

TODAY in the United States there is a new class of human beings who go by the name of Street People. They used to be confined to certain parts of the city, like the Bowery in New York, and Third and Howard Streets in San Francisco, but today they are increasingly mixed in with the rest. They lie along walls of buildings, among the passersby, sit over gratings for warmth, crouch in doorways. At meal times, unless too far gone, they line up where they know there will be food. Some are young enough, not badly dressed, and these may ask for money. But others are layered and encrusted with poverty going back many years, their hair coarse, sores on their lips, oblivious, asking nothing, muttering to themselves, carrying all their worldly goods in a soiled bag—as cut off from the passersby, as if they were a thousand miles away.

To the equivalent of these Street People 'Abdu'l-Bahá was a refuge and asylum, these that He nursed and fed. Except that the American ones have some access to government subsidies and charitable institutions, and live in relatively clean cities, while those children of His across the world often enough had no one but Him between them and death.

As Phelps tells it they were, many of them, blind,

were skin and bones, old, on crutches, of all the races thereabouts. ʿAbdu'l-Bahá would stand at a narrow angle of the street and call them to Him and greet them as friends. And to each He would say, "Welcome! Welcome! Well done! Well done!" They pushed about Him, grasped at Him, some even scratching and wounding His hands. There were five or six hundred poor in ʿAkká, and when winter came, the Master saw to it that each had a warm coat.

All this, while He Himself was poor and did not even belong to this country, His place of imprisonment and exile. Since 1892, He had been left in full charge of Bahá'u'lláh's Faith. When funds came in, He denied Himself, distributing all for the spread of the Cause, for the destitute, for the Household and their continual guests who flocked to Him even in the prison town, for the education of the young. (He financed the medical training in Beirut of both Yúnis Khán and H. Mu'ayyad.) When Ali-Kuli Khan served by ʿAbdu'l-Bahá's side virtually night and day for thirteen months as His amanuensis, the Master would give him exactly enough money for his needs—Khan never had to ask. Gifts of flowers, fruit, sweets, garments, were distributed, as were valuables such as jewels, unless these were necessary for the Faith. For example, when Elsa (Laura) Barney offered jewels to the Master, He gave them to Lua and Edward Getsinger in 1901 to pay for their journey back to the United States. Obviously, the Master did all this by putting everyone else first.

'ABDU'L-BAHÁ IN THE HOLY LAND
holding a Tablet

Phelps's book starts out with a typical scene, showing 'Abdu'l-Bahá in the midst of the crowding poor. Four years later, my mother, a young American woman, bride of Ali-Kuli Khan, witnessed much the same scene when she came on pilgrimage to 'Akká in 1906. The Master had directed her to wear the Persian veil in public, since times were dangerous, the Household was continually spied upon, and her husband was a Persian. Florence Khánum never really learned how to wear the *chádur*, but did her best. One day, wandering a little away from the Master's house and lost in her *chádur*, Florence found herself one with the crowd. That day, so it happened, 'Abdu'l-Bahá had appointed an attendant, Bashír, to give out the silver coins. Florence, struggling in vain to reach Bashír's protection and smothering in her costume, did not dare cry out or put aside her veil and reveal her American face. Terrified, pushing ahead, she was mistaken for a beggar woman trying to shove away the rest. Luckily, the believers who were assisting the harried Bashír realized who she was and, not without smiles, led her to safety.

Having been part of the beggar mob herself, Florence left a more horrified report than the genteel one of Myron Phelps. To her, New England-bred, these people were only half humans, with their wild staring eyes and soiled rags, their jutting bones, their injuries, their leprosy. To her they were hateful, like sick, ill-kept beasts.

To many, the poor still are. But not to 'Abdu'l-Bahá.

'ABDU'L-BAHÁ WITH SOME BELIEVERS

Taken in Haifa on March 3, 1921, on which day the Master started with Cummingham for Tiberias.

He went about His prison life, living the words of Bahá'u'lláh: "Know ye that the poor are the trust of God in your midst . . . betray not His trust." (*Gleanings*, p. 251) "If ye meet the abased or the down-trodden, turn not away disdainfully from them . . . Flee not from the face of the poor that lieth in the dust, nay rather befriend him." (*Ibid.*, p. 314) "Vaunt not thyself over the poor . . . " (*Hidden Words*, Arabic, 25)

And when 'Abdu'l-Bahá left the world in 1921, these and their descendants wailed that their Father was gone.

THE MASTER IN 'AKKÁ
by Myron H. Phelps

A VIEW OF LAKE GENNESARET, circa 1925

CHAPTER I

THE MASTER OF 'AKKÁ

SMALL as this world is, boast as we may of our means of communication, how little we really know of other lands; how slowly the actual thoughts, hopes, and aspirations of other peoples, the deep and real things of their lives, reach us, if they indeed ever reach us at all! We of the so-called "Christian" lands think, perhaps, that if Christ were to appear again upon the earth the good news would burden the telegraph, that His words and daily life would be marshalled forth under double headlines for our convenient perusal at breakfast or on the rapid-transit trains, giving us the interesting information without interrupting our important occupations. Ah no! We but deceive ourselves. The Man of Nazareth might pursue His holy life on the banks of the Jordan and the shores of Gennesaret* for a generation of men, but the faintest rumor of Him would not reach our ministers or our stockbrokers, our churches, or our exchanges.

*The Sea of Galilee. — ED.

I

Imagine that we are in the ancient house of the still more ancient city of 'Akká, which was for a month my home. The room in which we are faces the opposite wall of a narrow paved street, which an active man might clear at a single bound. Above is the bright sun of Palestine; to the right a glimpse of the old sea-wall and the blue Mediterranean. As we sit we hear a singular sound rising from the pavement, thirty feet below—faint at first, and increasing. It is like the murmur of human voices. We open the window and look down. We see a crowd of human beings with patched and tattered garments. Let us descend to the street and see who these are.

It is a noteworthy gathering. Many of these men are blind; many more are pale, emaciated, or aged. Some are on crutches; some are so feeble that they can barely walk. Most of the women are closely veiled, but enough are uncovered to cause us well to believe that, if the veils were lifted, more pain and misery would be seen. Some of them carry babes with pinched and sallow faces. There are perhaps a hundred in this gathering, and besides, many children. They are of all the races one meets in these streets—Syrians, Arabs, Ethiopians, and many others.

These people are ranged against the walls or seated on the ground, apparently in an attitude of expectation;—for what do they wait? Let us wait with them.

We have not to wait long. A door opens and a man comes out. He is of middle stature, strongly built. He wears flowing light-colored robes. On his head is a light buff fez with a white cloth wound about it. He is perhaps sixty years of age. His long grey hair rests on his shoulders. His forehead is broad, full, and high, his nose slightly aquiline, his moustaches and beard, the latter full though not heavy, nearly white. His eyes are grey and blue, large, and both soft and penetrating. His bearing is simple, but there is grace, dignity, and even majesty about his movements. He passes through the crowd, and as he goes utters words of salutation. We do not understand them, but we see the benignity and the kindliness of his countenance. He stations himself at a narrow angle of the street and motions to the people to come towards him. They crowd up a little too insistently. He pushes them gently back and lets them pass him one by one. As they come they hold their hands extended. In each open palm he places some small coins. He knows them all. He caresses them with his hand on the face, on the shoulders, on the head. Some he stops and questions. An aged Negro who hobbles up, he greets with some kindly inquiry; the old man's broad face breaks into a sunny smile, his white teeth glistening against his ebony skin as he replies. He stops a woman with a babe and fondly strokes the child. As they pass, some kiss his hand. To all he says, "*Marḥabá, marḥabá*" — "Well done, well done!"

So they all pass him. The children have been crowding around him with extended hands, but to them he has not given. However, at the end, as he turns to go, he throws a handful of coppers over his shoulder, for which they scramble.

During this time this friend of the poor has not been unattended. Several men wearing red fezes, and with earnest and kindly faces, followed him from the house, stood near him and aided in regulating the crowd, and now, with reverent manner and at a respectful distance, follow him away. When they address him they call him "Master."

This scene you may see almost any day of the year in the streets of 'Akká. There are other scenes like it, which come only at the beginning of the winter season. In the cold weather which is approaching, the poor will suffer, for, as in all cities, they are thinly clad. Some day at this season, if you are advised of the place and time, you may see the poor of 'Akká gathered at one of the shops where clothes are sold, receiving cloaks from the Master. Upon many, especially the most infirm or crippled, he himself places the garment, adjusts it with his own hands, and strokes it approvingly, as if to say, "There! Now you will do well." There are five or six hundred poor in 'Akká, to all of whom he gives a warm garment each year.

On feast days he visits the poor at their homes. He chats with them, inquires into their health and comfort, mentions by name those who are absent, and leaves gifts for all.

Nor is it the beggars only that he remembers. Those respectable poor who cannot beg, but must suffer in

A WELL NEAR THE MOSQUE IN 'AKKÁ

silence—those whose daily labor will not support their families—to these he sends bread secretly. His left hand knoweth not what his right hand doeth.

All the people know him and love him—the rich and the poor, the young and the old—even the babe leaping in its mother's arms. If he hears of any one sick in the city—Muslim or Christian, or of any other sect, it matters not—he is each day at their bedside, or sends a trusty messenger. If a physician is needed, and the patient poor, he brings or sends one, and also the necessary medicine. If he finds a leaking roof or a broken window menacing health, he summons a workman, and waits himself to see the breach repaired. If any one is in trouble,—if a son or a brother is thrown into prison, or he is threatened at law, or falls into any difficulty too heavy for him,—it is to the Master that he straightway makes appeal for counsel or for aid. Indeed, for counsel all come to him, rich as well as poor. He is the kind father of all the people.

This man who gives so freely must be rich, you think? No, far otherwise. Once his family was the wealthiest in all Persia.[1] But this friend of the lowly, like the Galilean, has been oppressed by the great. *For fifty years he and his family have been exiles and prisoners.* * Their property has been confiscated and wasted, and but little has been left to him. Now that he has not much he must spend little for himself that he may give

---

*'Abdu'l-Bahá was exiled from Iran with his father in 1853. This account was written in 1903, fifty years later. 'Abdu'l-Bahá remained a prisoner of the Ottoman Empire until 1908.—ED.

more to the poor. His garments are usually of cotton, and the cheapest that can be bought. Often his friends in Persia—for this man is indeed rich in friends, thousands and tens of thousands who would eagerly lay down their lives at his word—send him costly garments. These he wears once, out of respect for the sender; then he gives them away. A few months ago this happened. The wife of the Master* was about to depart on a journey. Fearing that her husband would give away his cloak and so be left without one for himself, she left a second cloak with her daughter, charging her not to inform her father of it. Not long after her departure, the Master, suspecting, it would seem, what had been done, said to his daughter, "Have I another cloak?" The daughter could not deny it, but told her father of her mother's charge. The Master replied, "How could I be happy having two cloaks, knowing that there are those that have none?" Nor would he be content until he had given the second cloak away.

He does not permit his family to have luxuries. He himself eats but once a day, and then bread, olives, and cheese suffice him.†

His room is small and bare, with only a matting on the stone floor. His habit is to sleep upon this floor. Not long ago a friend, thinking that this must be hard for a

---

*Munírih Khánum, the Holy Mother. —ED.

†'Abdu'l-Bahá preferred simple food, but it is an exaggeration to state that he invariably ate only once a day or that he limited his foods to those listed above. —ED.

man of advancing years, presented him with a bed fitted with springs and mattress. So these stand in his room also, but are rarely used. "For how," he says, "can I bear to sleep in luxury when so many of the poor have not even shelter?" So he lies upon the floor and covers himself only with his cloak.*

For more than thirty-four years this man has been a prisoner at 'Akká. But his jailors have become his friends. The governor of the city, the commander of the Army Corps, respect and honor him as though he were their brother. No man's opinion or recommendation has greater weight with them. He is the beloved of all the city, high and low. And how could it be otherwise? For to this man it is the law, as it was to Jesus of Nazareth, to do good to those who injure him. Have we yet heard of any one in lands which boast the name of Christ who lived that life?

Hear how he treats his enemies. One instance of many I have heard will suffice.

When the Master came to 'Akká there lived there a certain man from Afghanistan, an austere and rigid Mussulman. To him the Master was a heretic. He felt and nourished a great enmity towards the Master, and roused up others against him. When opportunity offered in gatherings of the people, as in the Mosque, he denounced him with bitter words.

"This man," he said to all, "is an impostor. Why do

---

*This is also perhaps an exaggeration. No other account of 'Abdu'l-Bahá's life indicates that he always slept on the floor in preference to the bed in his room. — ED.

8

'ABDU'L-BAHÁ

you speak to him? Why do you have dealings with him?" And when he passed the Master on the street he was careful to hold his robe before his face that his sight might not be defiled.

Thus did this Afghan. The Master, however, did thus: The Afghan was poor and lived in a mosque; he was frequently in need of food and clothing. The Master sent him both. These he accepted, but without thanks. He fell sick. The Master took him a physician, food, medicine, money. These, also, he accepted; but as he held out one hand that the physician might take his pulse, with the other he held his cloak before his face that he might not look upon the Master. *For twenty-four years* the Master continued his kindnesses and the Afghan persisted in his enmity. Then at last one day the Afghan came to the Master's door, and fell down, penitent and weeping, at his feet.

"Forgive me, sir!" he cried. "For twenty-four years I have done evil to you, for twenty-four years you have done good to me. Now I know that I have been in the wrong."

The Master bade him rise, and they became friends.

This Master is as simple as his soul is great. He claims nothing for himself—neither comfort, nor honor, nor repose. Three or four hours of sleep suffice him; all the remainder of his time and all his strength are given to the succor of those who suffer, in spirit or in body. "I am," he says, "the servant of God."

Such is 'Abbás Effendi, the Master of 'Akká.

BAHÍYYIH <u>KH</u>ÁNUM, THE GREATEST HOLY LEAF

CHAPTER II

THE STORY OF HIS LIFE

TEHRAN AND BAGHDAD

IN INTRODUCING 'Abbás Effendi to the reader I have thus far presented phases of his character which are unusual and first strike the attention. But these qualities are only the efflorescence of a strong, symmetrical, and well-balanced nature, which should be regarded from all sides. In the various relations of life when circumstances demand it he can be resolute, stern, and unyielding, as well as tender and compassionate. In his large family he is the firm and careful head, no less than the kind father and affectionate husband. Among men he is a strong and virile man, with a vigorous and clear intellect, a sound judgment, and substantial common sense. Among his people he is the executive, the administrator, and organizer of affairs.

Professor Browne, who visited 'Akká in 1890, thus graphically describes him as he saw him at that time (*A Traveller's Narrative*, Introduction, page xxxvi):

13

Seldom have I seen one whose appearance impressed me more. A tall strongly-built man holding himself straight as an arrow, with white turban and raiment, long black locks reaching almost to the shoulder, broad powerful forehead indicating a strong intellect combined with an unswerving will, eyes keen as a hawk's, and strongly marked but pleasant features — such was my first impression of 'Abbás Efendí, "the Master" (*Áká*) as he *par excellence* is called by the Bábís. Subsequent conversation with him served only to heighten the respect with which his appearance had from the first inspired me. One more eloquent of speech, more apt of illustration, more intimately acquainted with the sacred books of the Jews, the Christians, and the Muhammadans, could, I should think, scarcely be found even among the eloquent, ready, and subtle race to which he belongs. These qualities, combined with a bearing at once majestic and genial, made me cease to wonder at the influence and esteem which he enjoyed even beyond the circle of his father's followers. About the greatness of this man and his power no one who had seen him could entertain a doubt.

But the best estimate of the character of 'Abbás Effendi is to be gathered from the events of his life, to a brief narration of which I will now proceed. The story is told by Bahíyyih Khánum,* his sister, as follows:

"My brother, 'Abbás Effendi, now our Lord, was born at Tehran in the spring of 1844, at midnight following the day upon which, in the evening, the Báb made his declaration.† I was born three years later. He was therefore eight and I five, when in August, 1852, the attempt was made upon the life of the Shah of Persia by a young Bábí, who through ungoverned enthusiasm had

*The Greatest Holy Leaf. — ED.
†May 22, 1844. — ED.

14

lost his mental balance.[2] The events following this attempt are vividly impressed upon my mind. My mother, 'Abbás Effendi, myself, and my younger brother,* then a babe, were at the time in Tehran. My father was temporarily in the country.

"The attempted assassination caused great uproar and excitement throughout the city. All Bábís were searched for, and, when found, arrested. A mob sacked our house, stripping it of its furnishings. My mother fled with us to the home of a sister of her father, whose husband was an official of the government; but, seeing the alarm which her presence caused, she was unwilling to bring her relatives into danger, and returned to her own home.

"There we gathered together some furniture which had been left by the mob, and lived in one room, destitute of all but the barest necessities.

"My father, as my mother learned from a servant who was with him when he was arrested, was not long after brought to the city in chains and placed, with many other Bábís, in a dungeon† below ground.[3] They were chained together in squads by heavy chains passing about their necks. He expected to be executed first, as a leader, but he was instead reserved for the more horrible suffering of witnessing the successive torture and death of his companions separately. Each day one

*The Purest Branch, Mírzá Mihdí. — ED.
†Síyáh-Chál, the Black Pit. — ED.

15

NÁ$\underset{.}{S}$IRU'D-DÍN <u>SH</u>ÁH

or more were selected for this fate, and the others reminded that their turn might come tomorrow.

"Meanwhile, we heard each day the cries of the mob as a new victim was tortured or executed, not knowing but that it might be my father. My mother went daily to the house of her aunt for news of him and generally spent the entire day there, hoping that each hour would bring some tidings. These were long and weary days for my mother, young as she was and unaccustomed to sorrow.

"At first, on going to her aunt's, my mother would take me with her; but one day, returning unusually late, we found 'Abbás Effendi surrounded by a band of boys who had undertaken to personally molest him. He was standing in their midst as straight as an arrow—a little fellow, the youngest and smallest of the group—firmly but quietly *commanding* them not to lay their hands upon him, which, strange to say, they seemed unable to do. After that, my mother thought it unsafe to leave him at home, knowing his fearless disposition, and that when he went into the street, as he usually did to watch for her coming, eagerly expectant of news from his father for whom, even at that early age, he had a passionate attachment, he would be beset and tormented by the boys. So she took him with her, leaving me at home with my younger brother. I spent the long days in constant terror, cowering in the dark and afraid to unlock the door lest men should rush in and kill us.

"Meanwhile my mother was without money. She

WINTER IN TEHRAN, circa 1895

would have been reduced to extremities but for the fact that the buttons of our garments were of gold. These she used for buying food and for bribing the jailors to take food to my father.

"Four months passed in this fearful agony of suspense and terror. Meanwhile the government had investigated my father's case and had become convinced that he had had no connection with the attack upon the shah. This might not have been sufficient to effect his release at that time, on account of the popular fury against all Bábís, but he was so ill that it was thought he would die, and his illness was made a pretext for his liberation and he was released under surveillance.[4] Two weeks later, in company with a number of other families of believers, we set out for Baghdad with a military escort. It was bitterly cold, and the route lay over mountains. The journey lasted a month.[5] My father was very ill. The chains had left his neck galled, raw, and much swollen. My mother, who was pregnant, was unaccustomed to hardships, and was worried and harassed over our recent trials and the uncertainty of our fate. Another thing which grieved her was her separation from my younger brother whom, being very delicate, she had felt obliged to leave behind in Tehran as unfit to endure the hardships of this journey. We were all insufficiently clothed, and suffered keenly from exposure. My brother in particular was very thinly clad. Riding upon a horse, his feet, ankles, hands, and wrists were much exposed to the cold, which was so severe that they became frost-bitten and swollen and caused him great pain. The effects of this experience he feels to this day on being chilled or taking a cold.

"We arrived in Baghdad* in a state of great misery, and also of almost utter destitution. The only means that we had brought from Tehran consisted of a few personal effects that my mother had collected before our departure, which had been so hurried that she had had no time in which to make suitable preparation. Even these were nearly exhausted by the time we reached our destination, having been bartered on the journey for necessaries.

"More misery now stared us in the face. My father was still very ill; my mother and other women in delicate health; small children needed care, while our means were insufficient to procure even the usual necessities of life. My mother's health demanded that we should have servants, but we were unable to hire them. There were, indeed, those among the believers who would willingly have acted as such for us, and who actually did so, to some extent, but we could not permit them to do what we would not do ourselves — especially my mother, who was habitually very thoughtful and considerate, and who always preferred to work for herself and others rather than be a source of trouble to any one.

"I was, of course, too young to be of any real help;

*April 8, 1853. — ED.

20

A VIEW OF BAGHDAD, circa 1860

and as it was, there was no one in our household capable of doing much but my poor mother, who was unaccustomed to labor of any kind. In trying to wash our clothes her hands, which were fine and delicate, became blistered and were torn till they bled.

"In short, our sufferings—at least those of our own family—were indescribable. However, we struggled through this period as bravely as we could, until, after a time, occasional remittances came to us from Tehran, the proceeds of personal effects—jewels, cloth of gold, and other valuable articles which were a part of my mother's dowry—which had been left there to be sold. This money ameliorated our condition to a considerable extent.

"As soon as the Blessed Perfection* became some-what better, he began again to teach. Gathering the believers about him he encouraged, exhorted, and taught them until peace and happiness again reigned in the hearts of his devoted followers, and our little band of refugees found joy in his holy presence. But this happiness was of but brief duration. Not long after, my uncle, Ṣubḥ-i Azal,† my father's half brother, arrived

*This is the appellation usually given Bahá'u'lláh by Bahá'ís. —M.H.P.

†Morning of Eternity, a title used by Mírzá Yaḥyá. He eventually became the Arch-Breaker of the Covenant of the Báb, but at this time he was regarded by most Bábís as the head of the community. He had been nominated by the Báb, to "act solely as a figurehead pending the manifestation of the Promised One." (See *God Passes By*, pp. 28–29, 233.)—ED.

BAGHDAD
Showing the Tigris River.

in Baghdad, and then there began to be disharmony and misunderstandings among the believers. At the time of the trouble in Tehran, Ṣubḥ-i Azal had escaped and remained for some time in concealment. Then he followed us, traveling in the disguise of a dervish.

"I do not wish to be understood as asserting definitely that Ṣubḥ-i Azal was the cause of the discord to which I have referred; but it began at about the time of his joining us, and I myself have concluded that it was attributable to him.

"At length this state of affairs became very distasteful to my father, he being by nature a man of peace. Strife of any kind seemed to hurt him; more, however, because of the unhappiness which it brought upon others than because of the discomfort which it caused him. It was his habit, for the sake of peace and to quell strife, to take all blame upon himself where possible, and to seek to pacify those in contention by his love.

"After we had been in Baghdad about one year, he announced that he could endure it no longer, and that he would go away.

"Accordingly, taking a change of clothes, but no money, and against the entreaties of all the family, he set out. He was prevailed upon to take a servant, but sent him back the next day.*[6]

*Some of the details of this version of Bahá'u'lláh's departure to and return from Sulaymáníyyih differ from other historical accounts. The Greatest Holy Leaf was a child at the time these events took place and may not have been completely aware of all circumstances. —Ed.

"I have stated that my brother was deeply attached to his father; this attachment seemed to strengthen with his growth. After our father's departure he fell into great despondency. He would go away by himself, and, when sought for, be found weeping, often falling into such paroxysms of grief that no one could console him. His chief occupation at this time was copying and committing to memory the tablets* of the Báb. The childhood and youth of my brother was, in fact, in all respects unusual. He did not care for play or for amusement like other children. He would not go to school, nor would he apply himself to study. Horseback riding was the only diversion of which he was fond; in that he became proficient, being reputed to be a very skillful horseman.†

*The letters and shorter writings of the Báb, Bahá'u'lláh, and 'Abbás Effendi are called "tablets" by the Bahá'ís. — M.H.P.

†In reply to a question by Madame Canavarro, as to what he was most fond of as a child, 'Abbás Effendi said: "I cared more for hearing the tablets of the Báb recited than anything else. I used to commit them to memory and repeat them. This was the greatest pleasure I knew in my childhood — my play and amusement. I was not fond of study, nor did I care for books."

Being asked whether as a young man he did not seek amusement, like others of his age, he replied: "At Baghdad I rode on horseback; and at one time I had an idea that I would like to hunt. So on a certain occasion I joined a party of hunters and went with them to the chase. But when I saw them killing birds and animals, I thought that this could not be right. Then it occurred to me that better than hunting for animals, to kill them, was hunting for the souls of men to bring them to God. I then resolved that I would be a hunter of this sort. This was my first and last experience in the chase.

"This is all I want to tell you of myself. I am only a seeker of the souls of men, to guide them to God." — M.H.P.

"After my father's departure many months passed; he did not return, nor had we any word from him or about him. We were all in great sorrow, and made constant inquiries, hoping to hear some rumor which would enable us to trace him.

"There was an old physician at Baghdad who had been called upon to attend the family, and who had become our friend. He sympathized much with us, and undertook on his own account to make inquiries for my father. He at length thought that he had traced him to a certain locality, quite distant from Baghdad, in the mountains; and thereafter was accustomed to ask all persons whom he met from that region for such a man. These inquiries were long without definite result, but at length a certain traveler to whom he had described my father, said that he had heard of a man answering to that description, evidently of high rank, but calling himself a dervish, living in caves in the mountains. He was, he said, reputed to be so wise and wonderful in his speech on religious things that when people heard him they would follow him; whereupon, wishing to be alone, he would change his residence to a cave in some other locality. Further he related this incident: A boy attending a village school had been flogged and sent out for failure in his writing. While he was weeping outside the schoolroom, this holy man came by and asked the cause of his grief. When the lad had explained his trouble the dervish said: 'Do not grieve. I will set you another copy, and teach you to write well.' He then took the boy's

A DERVISH
with two young disciples, circa 1854

slate and wrote some words in very beautiful characters. The boy was delighted; and showing his slate in pride at now having a better master than he had had in the school, the people were astonished, dervishes being commonly illiterate. They then began to follow the dervish; who, wishing to meditate and pray in solitude, left that place for another.

"When we heard these things, we were convinced that this dervish was in truth our beloved one. But having no means to send him any word, or to hear further of him, we were very sad.

"There was then in Baghdad an earnest Bábí, formerly a pupil of Qurratu'l-'Ayn* (a woman famous for her beauty and learning, who was one of the disciples of the Báb, and a martyr). This man said to us that as he had no ties and did not care for his life, he desired no greater happiness than to be allowed to seek for him whom all loved so much, and that he would not return without him.†

"He was, however, very poor, not being able even to provide an ass for the journey; and he was besides not very strong, and therefore not able to go on foot. We had no money for the purpose, nor anything of value by the sale of which money could be procured, with the exception of a single rug, upon which we all slept. This

*Táhirih, one of the Letters of the Living appointed by the Báb. — ED.

†This man was Shaykh Sultán, who was accompanied by Javád-i Hattáb. — ED.

we sold and with the proceeds bought an ass for this friend, who thereupon set out upon the search.

"Time passed; we heard nothing, and fell into the deepest dejection and despair. Finally, four months having elapsed since our friend had departed, a message was one day received from him saying that he would bring my father home on the next day. The other members of the family could not credit the truth of this news, but it seemed to electrify my brother. He minutely questioned and examined the messenger, and became much excited. He quite believed that his father would return, but no one else did.

"During the night following the next day, however, my father walked into the house. We hardly knew him; his beard and hair were long and matted—he really was a dervish in appearance. The meeting between my brother and his father was the most touching and pathetic sight I have ever seen. 'Abbás Effendi threw himself on the floor before him and kissed and embraced his feet, weeping and crying, 'Why did you leave us, why did you leave us?' while the great uncouth dervish wept over his boy. The scene carried a weight not to be expressed in words.

"The absence of my father had covered a little more than two years.* After his return the fame which he had acquired in the mountains reached Baghdad, and

*Bahá'u'lláh left Baghdad on April 10, 1854, and returned on March 19, 1856. — ED.

not only Bábís but many others came to hear his teachings; and many, also, merely out of curiosity to see him. As he wished for retirement these curiosity seekers were a great trouble and annoyance to him. This aroused my brother and he declared that he would protect his father from such intrusions. Accordingly he prepared two placards, one for the door of his own room, which read, 'Those who come for information may apply within; those who come only because of curiosity had better stay away'; the other for the door of his father's room, of which the purport was, 'Let those who are searching for God come, and come, and come.' Then he announced that he himself would first see those who came. If he found that they were genuine truth-seekers he admitted them to his father's presence otherwise he did not permit them to see him.

"So time passed. My father taught many, and his followers became numerous. Many of them were the fierce and untutored Arabs of Iraq. All evinced an intense devotion to him. He was visited also by many Bábís from Persia.

"During these years 'Abbás Effendi was accustomed to frequent the mosques and argue with the doctors and learned men. They were astonished at his knowledge and acumen, and he came to be known as the youthful sage. They would ask him, 'Who is your teacher— where do you learn the things which you say?' His reply was that his father had taught him. Although he had

'ABDU'L-BAHÁ AS A YOUNG MAN

never been a day in school, he was as proficient in all that was taught as well-educated young men, which was the cause of much remark among those who knew him.

"In appearance my brother was at this time a remarkably fine-looking youth. He was noted as one of the handsomest young men in Baghdad."

CONSTANTINOPLE circa 1863

CHAPTER III

THE STORY OF HIS LIFE (*Continued*)

CONSTANTINOPLE AND ADRIANOPLE

"THE GOVERNOR of Baghdad at this time was a relative of my father, but his enemy on account of differences in religous opinion and family misunderstandings.⁷ This man, rendered uncomfortable by the sight of my father's increasing fame and influence, exerted himself to effect his removal from Baghdad. He caused representations to be made to the Shah of Persia that, whereas Bahá'u'lláh had been driven out of Persia because of the harm threatened by his presence to the Muhammadan religion in that country, now he was injuring the religion even more in Baghdad, and still exerting his evil influence in Persia; and that therefore he ought to be removed to a place at a greater distance from that country, and one where he could do less harm.

"These representations and suggestions he sent repeatedly to the Court of Persia, until at length the shah was moved to use his influence with the Sultan of

Turkey to have the Bábís transferred from Baghdad to Constantinople. An order to this effect was at length made by the sultan.

"When this news came to us, from which we inferred that my father would again be made a prisoner, we were thrown into consternation, fearing another separation. He was summoned before the magistrates. My brother imperiously declared that he would go in his stead; but this our father overruled, and went himself.[8] Great numbers of his followers had assembled about our house, and these witnessed his departure with many demonstrations of grief, feeling that it was possible that he might not return.

"The magistrates expressed great sorrow to my father; they said that they respected and loved him, that they had not instigated the order, but that they were powerless to suspend or modify it, and must proceed with its execution. My father remained in conference with them nearly all day, but could do nothing to avert the catastrophe.[9] When he returned, he told us that we must prepare to set out for Constantinople in two weeks.

"This report was like a death-knell to his followers, who were still gathered about the house. Many of them were Arabs; their fierce natures rebelled and they gave way to violent remonstrances. They implored the Blessed Perfection not to desert them. 'You are our shepherd,' they said; 'without you we must die.'

"The next day they so overran the house that we

BOATS IN BAGHDAD
unloading on the banks of the Tigris, circa 1925.

could not prepare for the journey. Then the Blessed Perfection proposed to go with 'Abbás Effendi to the garden of one of our friends* and live there in a tent till the time of departure, that the family might be able to proceed with the packing. This remark was repeated and misunderstood, and the rumor circulated among the believers that the Blessed Perfection was to be taken away alone. Then they came pouring in by hundreds, so wild with grief that they could not be pacified; and when my father started to leave the house with my brother they threw themselves upon the ground before him. One man who had an only child, which had come to him late in his life, stripped the clothes from the child's body and placing it at my father's feet cried, 'Naked I give you my child, my precious child, to do with as you will; only promise not to leave us in distress. Without you we cannot live.'

"Then, as the only way in which to soothe his followers, the Blessed Perfection took all his family to the garden, leaving to friends the preparation of his household goods for the journey. Here we pitched tents and lived in them for two weeks.† The tents made, as it were, a little village, that of my father, which he occupied alone, in the center.

"Four days before the caravan was to set out, the

---

*The Najíbíyyih Garden, now known to Bahá'ís as the Garden of Ridván. — ED.

†Actually, twelve days. This period is now celebrated each year by Bahá'ís as the Festival of Ridván, April 21 to May 2. — ED.

Blessed Perfection called 'Abbás Effendi into his tent and told him that he himself was the one whose coming had been promised by the Báb—the Chosen of God, the Center of the Covenant. A little later, and before leaving the garden, he selected from among his disciples four others, to whom he made the same declaration. He further said to these five that for the present he enjoined upon them secrecy as to this communication, as the time had not come for a public declaration; but that there were reasons which caused him to deem it necessary to make it at that time to a few whom he could trust.[10] These reasons he did not state; but they are to my mind suggested by the subsequent events which I shall narrate farther on, and which I think he at that time anticipated, and in view of which he felt that he needed special protection.

"Many of the Blessed Perfection's followers decided to abandon Baghdad also, and accompany him in his wanderings. When the caravan started, our company numbered about seventy-five persons. All the young men, and others who could ride, were mounted on horses.[11] The women and the Blessed Perfection were furnished wagons. We were accompanied by a military escort. This journey took place in 1863, about eleven years after our arrival in Baghdad.

"From the time when the declaration was made to him at Baghdad, Abbás Effendi seemed to constitute himself the special attendant, servant, and body-guard of his father. He guarded him day and night on this

39

A CARAVAN

showing howdahs on the backs of horses.

journey, riding by his wagon and watching near his tent. He thus had little sleep, and, being young, became extremely weary. His horse was Arab and very fine, and so wild and spirited that no other man could mount him, but under my brother's hand as gentle and docile as a lamb. In order to get a little rest, he adopted the plan of riding swiftly a considerable distance ahead of the caravan, when, dismounting and causing his horse to lie down, he would throw himself on the ground and place his head on his horse's neck. So he would sleep until the cavalcade came up, when his horse would awake him by a kick and he would remount.

"The march to Constantinople occupied four months.* Much of the weather was inclement and during many whole days we were without proper food. In our company were many small children, upon whom and the women the journey was very hard. On one occasion during a long and cold march, my brother having obtained some bread, rice, and milk, my father made up with his own hands a sort of pudding by boiling these together with a little sugar, which was then distributed to all. The preparation of this food was a reminiscence of my father's two-years' sojourn in the mountains, where he was dependent on what might be given him, and this dish—which he sometimes made for himself— was the only warm food he had.

*Bahá'u'lláh and His company left Baghdad on May 3, 1863, and arrived in Constantinople on August 16, 1863.—ED.

41

"Such times as these were moments of pleasure; but there was always present a feeling of apprehension—as though a sword were hanging over our heads.

"Arrived in Constantinople we found ourselves prisoners.[12] We were put into a small house, the men below and the women above. My father and his family were given two rooms. The weather was very cold and damp, and we had no fires or proper clothing. Because of the crowding the atmosphere was foul. We petitioned for better quarters, and were given another house, which was to some extent an improvement.

"While we were here the Blessed Perfection was advised by persons of prominence who came to see him to appeal to the sultan, state his case, and demand justice, in accordance with the Turkish custom. To these suggestions he replied that he was a man whose only concern was the spiritual welfare of men; that he had never interfered in any way with worldly affairs, nor should he ever do so, even in his own behalf; that the sultan had commanded his presence in Constantinople, and for that reason alone he had come; that in like manner he should in the future comply with the wishes of the sultan; that he saw no reason why he, a spiritual man, should initiate the trouble, argument, and commotion incident to an appeal; and that if the government wished to investigate the truth of the matter, it would itself institute an inquiry.

"I have heard that these words were repeated to the

SOME BAHÁ'ÍS IN CONSTANTINOPLE
Áqáy-i Kalím (Mírzá Músá), center, with (l. to r.) Hájí Mírzá
Ahmad of Kashan, Áqá Muhammad-Sadiq of Isfahan, Nabíl-i
Zarandí, and Sayyid Muhammad of Isfahan.

CONSTANTINOPLE,
Overlooking the Bosporus, circa 1890.

A STREET IN CONSTANTINOPLE, circa 1890

SULṬÁN ʿABDUʾL-ʿAZÍZ OF TURKEY

sultan and did not please him, perhaps because a different construction had been put upon them by the narrator than the meaning which the Blessed Perfection intended to convey. However that may be, it being a matter about which I cannot speak with certainty, my father was not called upon to appear at any inquiry. An order was, however, made, about two months after our arrival in Constantinople, directing our transfer to Adrianople [Edirne], a town in eastern European Turkey of notoriously bad climate, to which criminals were often sent.[13]

"Before we set out a threat was made of separating us — of sending the Blessed Perfection to one place, his family to another, and his followers elsewhere. This overwhelmed us with apprehension, which hung over us and tormented us during the whole of the journey and long after. The dread of this or of the execution of my father was the greatest of our trials — a horrible fear of unknown danger always menacing us. Such threats were frequently repeated after this time also. Had it not been for them we could have borne our sufferings with greater resignation; but these kept us always in a heart-sickening suspense.

"The journey to Adrianople, although occupying but nine days, was the most terrible experience of travel we had thus far had.[14] It was the beginning of winter, and very cold; heavy snow fell most of the time; and destitute as we were of proper clothing or food, it was a miracle that we survived it. We arrived at Adrianople all sick—even the young and strong. My brother again had his feet frozen on this journey.

"Our family, numbering eleven persons, was lodged in a house of three rooms just outside the city of Adrianople.[15] It was like a prison; without comforts and surrounded by a guard of soldiers. Our only food was the prison fare allowed us, which was unsuitable for the children and the sick.

"That winter was a period of intense suffering, due to cold, hunger, and, above all, to the torments of vermin, with which the house was swarming. These made even the days horrible, and the nights still more so. When they were so intolerable that it was impossible to sleep, my brother would light a lamp (which somewhat intimidated the vermin) and by singing and laughing seek to restore the spirits of the family.

"In the spring, on the appeal of the Blessed Perfection to the governor, we were removed to somewhat more comfortable quarters within the city. Our family was given the second story of a house, of which some of the believers occupied the ground floor.[16]

"We remained for five years in Adrianople.* The Blessed Perfection resumed his teaching and gathered about him a large following. We were very poor and always in great privation, but had become so inured to suffering that we should have lived in tolerable contentment had it not been for two things—the feeling of

*From December 12, 1863, to August 12, 1868. — ED.

A STREET ON THE OUTSKIRTS OF ADRIANOPLE

dread and sense of unknown danger of which I have before spoken, and another matter to which I will presently more particularly refer.

"During this period, as, in fact, had been the case for a number of years, 'Abbás Effendi was the chief dependence and comfort of the entire family. He had from childhood a remarkably self-sacrificing nature, habitually yielding his own wishes and giving up whatever he had to his brothers and sisters, keeping nothing for himself. He was always gentle; never became angry, and never retaliated. The life we were living afforded constantly recurring occasions for the exhibition of these qualities of his character; and his unceasing efforts did a great deal to make its conditions endurable for the other members of the family.

"For the poor also he had ever been very tender-hearted, and, destitute as we were, he always contrived to find something to give to others who were in greater want. This almsgiving proclivity of my brother was a great trial to our mother, for in our straitened circumstances she found it very difficult with the means at her disposal to provide for her own family only those things which were actually necessary.

"The matter to which I have just referred as interfering with our contentment was a very terrible experience brought upon us by Subh-i Azal, to whose machinations our subsequent sufferings were chiefly due, and which were the immediate cause of our being sent some years later from Adrianople to 'Akká. To this very serious affair I will now proceed.

A GROUP PHOTO OF SOME BAHÁ'ÍS
in exile in Adrianople.

'ABDU'L-BAHÁ (seated center) AND THE PUREST BRANCH (to his left) with some of the believers in Adrianople.

"Ṣubḥ-i Azal continued to be one of our company after we came to Baghdad in 1853. With his family he now occupied in Adrianople a house separate from ours though near it. The relations between the two families, which for a time while we were in Baghdad had been strained, had become again harmonious. The food of Ṣubḥ-i Azal's family was usually prepared in our house, under my supervision, and sent to Ṣubḥ-i Azal's house. The reason for this was that his wives were not properly attentive to their household affairs and prepared his food so badly that it was not suitable for him to eat. We saw this, and, in order to enable him to live comfortably, offered to cook his food and send it to him.

"There was a bath in our house, but none in Ṣubḥ-i Azal's, and he was accustomed to use our bath. The same servant* prepared the bath and acted as bath attendant for both my father and Ṣubḥ-i Azal.

"Up to this time the declaration which the Blessed Perfection had made to five of his disciples in Baghdad had not been formally communicated to Ṣubḥ-i Azal, or, indeed, to any one else, and we do not know that he was aware of it: though his conduct suggests that he suspected it, and that this suspicion furnished the incentive which prompted him in doing what I am about to relate.[17] As you no doubt know, Ṣubḥ-i Azal claimed to have been appointed by the Báb as his successor, and therefore to be, after the Báb's death, the head of the Bábí Church. [18]

*Ustád Muḥammad-'Alíy-i Salmání, the Barber. — ED.

"The events which I am about to relate occurred about one year after he had moved into the city from the quarters which he had at first occupied in Adrianople. One day while in the bath Ṣubḥ-i Azal remarked to the servant (who was a believer) that the Blessed Perfection had enemies and that in the bath he was much exposed, and asked whether it would not be easy for an attendant who was not faithful to the Blessed Perfection to make away with him while shaving him. The servant replied that this was certainly the case. Ṣubḥ-i Azal then asked him whether, if God should lay upon him the command to do this, he would obey it. The servant understood this question, coming from Ṣubḥ-i Azal, to be a suggestion of such a command, and was so terrified by it that he rushed screaming from the room. He first met 'Abbás Effendi and repeated to him Ṣubḥ-i Azal's words.[19] My brother endeavored to quiet him, and commanded his silence. This the servant refused unless he was taken at once to the Blessed Perfection. 'Abbás Effendi accordingly accompanied him to my father, who listened to his story and then enjoined absolute silence upon him.

"This occurrence was ignored by my father and brother, and our relations with Ṣubḥ-i Azal continued to be cordial. The Blessed Perfection was indeed several times warned to beware of Ṣubḥ-i Azal, by persons who claimed to have overheard conversations between him and his intimates, but no attention was paid to these warnings.

ṢUBḤ-I AZAL, MÍRZÁ YAḤYÁ
in later years.

USTÁD MUHAMMAD-'ALÍY-I SALMÁNÍ
barber and bath attendant to Bahá'u'lláh.

"Some time afterwards, to celebrate a family festival day, Ṣubḥ-i Azal invited us all to his house. At this time, also, my father was warned not to take food there, but replied that he must treat Ṣubḥ-i Azal with kindness and could not refuse it.

"This entertainment was looked upon as cementing the family reconciliation, and it is usual on such occasions among Persians for the heads of the two family factions which have been alienated to eat from the same plate. So, now, rice for both my father and Ṣubḥ-i Azal was served to them on one plate. This rice, as well as all the other food used for the meal, had been prepared in Ṣubḥ-i Azal's house, contrary to the usual custom. Now my father and Ṣubḥ-i Azal had these well-known peculiarities of taste—that the former was very fond of onions, while the latter could not endure them. The portion of rice intended for my father was accordingly flavored with onions, while that intended for Ṣubḥ-i Azal was differently prepared. The servant bringing in the plate placed it, at the direction of Ṣubḥ-i Azal, with the side upon which was the rice flavored with onions toward the Blessed Perfection. While he did so Ṣubḥ-i Azal smilingly remarked, 'Here is rice cooked as you like it!' My father ate some of the rice prepared for him, but fortunately not very much, as for some reason it did not please him. He preferred the rice prepared for Ṣubḥ-i Azal, and ate of it, and also of the dishes which the others at the table were eating.[20]

57

A PERSIAN MEAL

"Soon after eating the rice my father became ill and went home. About midnight he was seized with severe vomiting and passing of blood from the bowels. A physician was summoned, and declared that he had been poisoned.

"My father was desperately ill for twenty-two days; during all this time he took no food. On the eighteenth day the physician said that he could not live. The death sentence terribly moved 'Abbás Effendi. He placed his head on the pillow beside his father's in the utmost agony of grief. He implored him to live for the sake of the world, for his family, and for him. My father was too feeble to speak, and could only place his hand on my brother's head. The physician was deeply moved by the sight. He had learned to love 'Abbás Effendi,—as did every one who came in contact with him,—and declared he would give his life to save the father for the boy. Thrice he repeated, 'I will give my life—I will give my life—I will give my life,' walking as he spoke several times around the bed. At length, utterly despairing of the case, he left. The next morning he sent word that he was ill, and advised that another physician be summoned. Nine days later he died. We then recalled his singular words.[21]

"Meanwhile we did not summon another physician for my father, feeling that the case was hopeless; but to our surprise his condition soon showed marked improvement, and on the third day he asked for food, which gave us much hope. From this time he grew stronger continuously, but very slowly,* and at length recovered.

"After the recovery of my father from this illness, 'Abbás Effendi strongly urged him to declare himself to Ṣubḥ-i Azal. My father, however, persisted in replying that so long as Ṣubḥ-i Azal did not effect other harm than he was able to do to him personally, that is, so long as he did not injure the Cause, he would not assert himself against him.

"Ṣubḥ-i Azal made no further attempts upon the life of the Blessed Perfection, but he began to endeavor to arouse dissensions among the believers, making various false accusations against the Blessed Perfection. At this

*Partisans of Ṣubḥ-i Azal have endeavored to anticipate and break the force of these revelations by publishing the following story, cited by Professor Browne in a note, *A Traveller's Narrative*, p. 359. They allege that Bahá'u'lláh "caused poison to be placed in one side of the dish of food which was to be set before himself and Ṣubḥ-i Azal, giving instructions that the poisoned side should be turned towards his brother. As it happened, however, the food had been flavored with onions, and Ṣubḥ-i Azal, disliking this flavor, refused to partake of the dish; but the poison having diffused itself to some extent through the whole mass, he was presently attacked with vomiting and other symptoms of poisoning." This transparent fabrication assumes an impossible ignorance on the part of Bahá'u'lláh of the fact that onions were disliked by his brother, as well as the improbable hypothesis that Bahá'u'lláh would knowingly have partaken of food in which poison had been placed.
In the following pages of his book Professor Browne mentions a number of other charges made against Bahá'u'lláh by the Azalís, equally incredible, at least so it seems to me, to anyone familiar with the character and teachings of the Bahá'ís. I do not think that it would be time well employed to advert to these charges in detail. Allegations so flatly in contradiction to the spirit, lives, and

time, of course, the Bábís in general did not know that my father had said that he was the Divine Manifestation, but he was regarded by most of them as their leader, and very much beloved. Ṣubḥ-i Azal was looked upon as a leader, however, by some of the Bábís.

"Thus matters went, becoming worse and worse, until it was plainly evident that the Cause was suffering. Then the Blessed Perfection summoned 'Abbás Effendi and said to him that the time had come for a public declaration. 'Not for myself would I do it,' he said, 'but because the welfare of the Cause demands it.' He then wrote a tablet,* longer than any he had before written and of great power,—it has been said that men trembled as they read it,—addressed to the Bábís generally, and setting forth his declaration.

"This tablet he directed to be read to every Bábí, but first of all to Ṣubḥ-i Azal. He assigned to one of his followers the duty of taking it to Ṣubḥ-i Azal, reading

---

teachings of Bahá'u'lláh and his successor, will quickly enough fade away and be forgotten if left to themselves. But I must protest most energetically against Professor Browne's suggestion (pp. 371 *et seq.*) that any traits of Oriental character shared by the leaders of Bahaism could be assumed as possibly closing their eyes to the iniquity of such proceedings in support of their cause. Of course one cannot dogmatize on impressions of character, but I wish to place on record the fact that my own acquaintance with the Bahá'ís and the spirit which animates them makes it inconceivable to me that such utter perversion of moral sense, however possible it may generally be to the Oriental type of character, about which I here express no opinion, could under any circumstances characterize their policy as a body, or the policy of their leaders.—M.H.P.

*The Súriy-i Amr.—ED.

61

it to him, and returning with Ṣubḥ-i Azal's reply. When Ṣubḥ-i Azal had heard the tablet, he did not attempt to refute it; on the contrary he accepted it, and said that it was true. But he went on to maintain that he himself was co-equal with the Blessed Perfection, affirming that he had had a vision on the previous night in which he had received this assurance.[22]

"When this statement of Ṣubḥ-i Azal was reported to the Blessed Perfection, the latter directed that every Bábí should be informed of it at the time when he heard his own tablet read. This was done, and much uncertainty resulted among the believers. They generally applied to the Blessed Perfection for advice, which, however, he declined to give. At length he told them that he would seclude himself from them for four months, and that during this time they must decide the question for themselves.

"This he did. None of the believers other than his own family had access to him, or communication with him, for four months.[23] At the end of that period all the Bábís in Adrianople, with the exception of Ṣubḥ-i Azal and five or six others, came to the Blessed Perfection and declared that they accepted him as the Divine Manifestation, whose coming the Báb had foretold. The Bábís of Persia, Syria, Egypt, and other countries, also, in due time accepted the Blessed Perfection with substantial unanimity.*

*Ṣubḥ-i Azal had, indeed, a few adherents; but his following has been so inconsiderable, and so utterly without the vitality and power

"Subh-i Azal now took up another line of action. He opened a correspondence with prominent persons in the Turkish government and the Muslim Church, in which he alleged that the Blessed Perfection was stirring up strife and seeking to destroy the Muslim faith by show-ing a contempt for the Qur'án, neglecting the fast of Ramadan, permitting the women of his followers to go unveiled, condemning polygamy, and the like. These allegations, although wholly unfounded, since the Blessed Perfection, equally with our Master at the pres-ent time, required of his followers the most careful observance of, and respect for, the social customs of the people among whom they lived, were persisted in by Subh-i Azal, until he had made the impression which he desired. The Turkish government, annoyed and ir-ritated, finding our people, between whom, as can be well understood, it was unable to discriminate, vex-atious and troublesome, wearied of the whole matter, and determined to scatter us; a course which under the circumstances was a quite natural and intelligible out-come of Subh-i Azal's actions.[24] An order was there-fore issued decreeing that the Bábís in Adrianople should be separated and banished; that Subh-i Azal should be sent to one place, the Blessed Perfection to another, his family to another, and the followers to still

of assimilation so characteristic equally of the earliest and latest stages of this movement, that the defection has not impaired in any ascertainable degree its solidarity, and is to be regarded, in con-sidering the present status of the faith, as a quite negligible quan-tity. — M.H.P.

others; and that all should be kept in ignorance of their own and the others' destinations.

"During the period of his residence at Adrianople, 'Abbás Effendi had endeared himself to every one, high and low, those of the faith and others alike. He taught much and even at that time was commonly called the 'Master.' The governor himself had become a friend of the Master's and delighted to listen to his religious discourses. It was the habit of the governor frequently to have the Master at the palace, and when my brother could not go to the governor he sometimes came to my brother.

"When the governor received the order of banishment from Adrianople he was so affected by it that, not having the heart to execute it himself, he put it into the hands of his subordinates for execution, wrote a letter to 'Abbás Effendi, and left the city. In this letter he said:

"'This trouble has come upon you through members of your own family. It is Ṣubḥ-i Azal who has caused the sultan to take these steps. I am powerless to aid you, and my love for you is so great that I must go away. I cannot see this dreadful thing happen.'

"This trouble broke with the suddenness of a tornado upon us. We were sitting quietly together at home when we heard a bugle-call. My brother looked out and saw a cordon of soldiers about the house presenting arms. Our first thought was that the life of the Blessed

Perfection or of 'Abbás Effendi was threatened. The latter endeavored to quiet our alarm, and went out to inquire the cause of this demonstration. He was given the governor's letter. The family consulted and 'Abbás Effendi then told the officer in command that we would die rather than be separated, and asked at least for respite. The reply was, 'No; you must go today, Bahá'u'lláh and his family to different places, and neither can know the destination of the other.' 'Abbás Effendi demanded permission to go to the governor's palace and appeal to his representative. This was at first refused but finally granted, and he set out between two guards.

"My brother pleaded so eloquently with the officials that they consented to telegraph to Constantinople asking that the order be changed so that our family might remain together. A reply was received refusing the change. My brother persisted, and had such influence with the officials that they seemed unable to put the measure into execution, permitting him to send despatch after despatch for a week.

"These were days of horror. The members of our family neither ate nor slept. No cooking was done in the house. When my brother left in the morning with the guards we feared that we might never see him again, and watched hour after hour for his return.

"At length a telegram was received granting the concession that my father should be permitted to take with him his immediate family, but directing that his followers should be separated from him, without knowledge of his destination. A servant who had accompanied my brother overheard a part of this despatch read and misunderstood it. Without waiting to inquire whether he had heard aright, he returned to us with the report that the first order was not to be rescinded; that the Blessed Perfection was to be separated from his family and his followers. After telling us this he ran out and spread the news among the believers who were gathered near our house. They were as though stunned, paralysed. One of them, an old and faithful follower,* seized a knife, and exclaiming, 'If I must be separated from my Lord, I will go now and join my God,' cut his throat. Fortunately this man's knife was partially arrested by a bystander so that his jugular vein was not severed; with the aid of a physician his life was ultimately saved.[25]

"The attempted suicide caused a great noise and disturbance, which attracted our attention. My mother and I went out to inquire into the cause of the commotion. We came near, and saw a man lying on the ground with blood streaming from him. The soldiers surrounding the group prevented us from approaching closely enough to determine with certainty who it was, but the first thought which came to us was that my poor brother, on hearing that the order was to be carried out,

*Hájí Ja'fár-i Tabrízí. — Ed.

had, in his despair, killed himself. We could hear the gulping utterances of the man—'You have separated me from my Lord,—I prefer to die.' Though unable to distinguish the voice, we still thought it was my brother. We remained in this agonizing suspense for some time, until we suddenly heard my brother's voice rising high above the din, and speaking with tremendous force.

"On hearing him, two things amazed us. First, he seemed to be wrought up to the highest pitch of anger and indignation. Never before had we heard him speak an angry word. We had known him sometimes impatient and preemptory, but never angry. And then, his great excitement had apparently given him command of the Turkish language, which no one had ever heard him speak before.* He was, in Turkish, and in the most impassioned and vehement manner, protesting against, and denouncing, the treatment of the officers and demanding the presence of the governor, who in the meantime had returned to the city. The officers seemed cowed by his vehemence, and the governor was sent for. He came, and seeing the situation said, 'It is impossible, we cannot separate these people.'

"The governor returned to his palace and telegraphed

---

*'Abdu'l-Bahá had lived in Turkish territory since 1853, when the Holy Family was banished to Baghdad. Since he had regular dealings with the Ottoman authorities during most of this time, it is likely that he had acquired a knowledge of the Turkish language. However, he may have had no occasion to use it in the presence of the women of the Household before this incident. — ED.

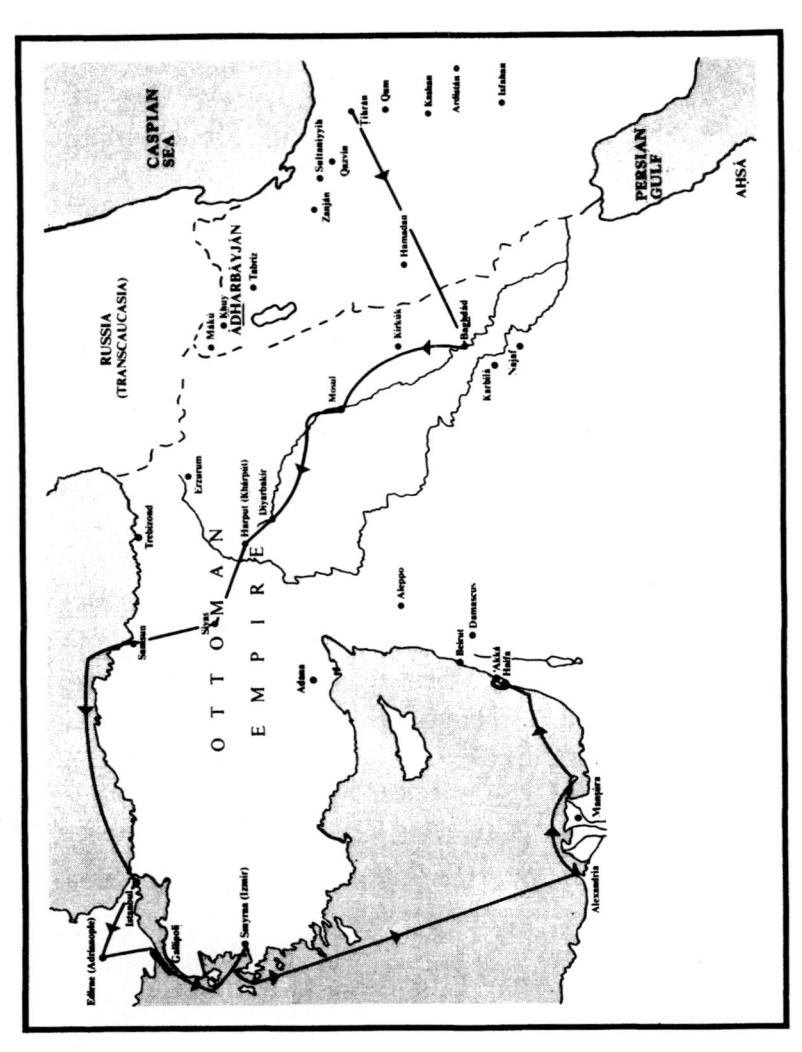

MAP OF THE EXILES OF BAHÁ'U'LLÁH

to Constantinople. The next day he received a reply granting permission to the followers of the Blessed Perfection to accompany him. We were told to prepare for immediate departure, but were not told to what place we were to be sent. When we set out there were seventy-seven in all in our band. We journeyed six days, and arrived at Gallipoli, which is on the sea.[26]

"On our arrival at this town we were met with the information that the governor had a telegraphic order from the sultan's government directing our separation; that my father with one servant was to go to one place, my brother with one servant to another, the family to Constantinople, the other followers to various places. This sudden and unexplained withdrawal of the hard-won concession we had so recently obtained exhausted our patience. We unhesitatingly declared that we would not be separated, and a repetition, in substance, of the events of the last days in Adrianople followed. My brother went to the governor and told him that we would not submit to separation. 'Do this,' said he, — 'take us out on a steamer and drown us in the ocean. You can thus end at once our sufferings and your perplexities. But we refuse to be separated.'

"We remained in Gallipoli for a week, in the same horrible suspense which we had experienced at Adrianople.[27] Finally my brother, by his eloquence in argument and power of will, succeeded in gaining for the second time from the Constantinople government the concession that we should remain together.[28]

69

"At Gallipoli the German, Russian, and English consuls called upon the Blessed Perfection and offered to intercede in his behalf with the Turkish government, assuring him that they could procure, for him and his family, permission to go to one of the countries of Western Europe, where they would have no further trouble.[29] My father replied that he did not wish to oppose the will of the sultan, nor would he consent to abandon his followers; that his only interests were in spiritual things and his only desire to preach a religion, and that therefore he had nothing to fear.

"The order from Constantinople directed that we should embark together upon a government vessel, and no time was lost in putting it into execution. In the hurry, distress, and uncertainty of the moment, we neglected to provide food for the voyage, but to one old servant, on his way to the ship, the thought occurred that he had not seen any provisions prepared, and he bought a box of bread. This, with the ship's prisoners' rations, which were almost inedible, was the only food we had for five days, when we reached Alexandria. Here the rumor that we were to be separated was renewed; and all were so terrified by it that no one was willing to leave the ship to buy provisions lest he be prevented from returning.[30] We were able to procure only some grapes and mineral water.

"The little bread we had was now spoiled; and, what with hunger, fright, and grief, we were almost bereft of

THE PORT OF ALEXANDRIA, circa 1870.

reason. On one of our company,* indeed, these conditions had so preyed as to unbalance his mind, and he
threw himself from the ship as we were leaving the har-
bor of Alexandria.[31] The ships' officers were, however,
fortunately able to bring her to in time to reach this
man before he sank, and he was brought on board and
revived."

*Áqá 'Abdu'l-Ghaffár-i Iṣfahání. — ED.

'AKKÁ, circa 1925

CHAPTER IV

THE STORY OF HIS LIFE (*Continued*)

'AKKÁ

"AFTER a voyage of about two days we were landed at Haifa, in Syria. All were sick, from hunger or eating improper food. I myself was a healthy woman up to the time of taking this voyage; since then I have never been well.

"We remained one day in the prison at Haifa, the men in chains, and were then taken in small boats to 'Akká (a distance of ten miles).[32] The water was very rough, and nearly all became seasick.

"'Akká, as we afterwards learned, was a prison to which the worst criminals were commonly sent from all parts of the Turkish Empire. It was reported to have a deadly climate. There was a saying that if a bird flew over 'Akká it would fall and die.

"At that time there was no landing for the city: it was necessary to wade ashore from the boats. The governor ordered that the women be carried on the backs of the men. My brother was not willing that this should be

75

done, and protested against it. He was one of the first to land, and procured a chair, in which, with the help of one of the believers, he carried the women ashore. The Blessed Perfection was not allowed to leave his boat until all his family had landed. When he had come ashore, the family were counted and taken to the army barracks, in which we were to be imprisoned. From the terrible sufferings and privations of the journey we were nearly all sick; worst of all, perhaps, the Blessed Perfection and myself.

"Arrived at the barracks, it was proposed to put the Blessed Perfection and his family on the second floor, and he was sent up; but I fainted from exhaustion and was unable to ascend the stairs. [Here the narrator paused a moment, visibly trembling, and then continued.] Of my own experience perhaps this is the most awful. The horrible sufferings of the voyage had reduced me almost to the point of death. Upon that came the seasickness. When we landed in 'Akká all the people of the town came crowding about us, talking loudly in Arabic, which I understood. Some said that we were to be put in the dungeons and chained; others that we were to be thrown into the sea. The most horrible jests and jeers were hurled at us as we were marched through the streets to this dreadful prison.

"Imagine, if you can, the overpowering impression made by all this upon the mind of a young girl, such as I was then. Can you wonder that I am serious, and that my life is different from those of my countrywomen? But this is digressing.

'AKKÁ, THE SEA GATE

"When we had entered the barracks the massive door was closed upon us and the great iron bolts thrown home. I cannot find words to describe the filth and stench of that vile place. We were nearly up to our ankles in mud in the room into which we were led. The damp, close air and the excretions of the soldiers combined to produce horrible odors. Then, being unable to bear more, I fainted. As I fainted, those about me caught me before I fell; but because of the mud and filth there was no place upon which I could be laid. On one side of the room was a man weaving a mat for the soldiers. One of our friends took this mat and I was placed upon it. Then they begged for water, but they could not get it. The soldiers would permit no one to go out. There was a pool of water on the dirt floor, in which the mat-maker had been moistening his rushes. Some of this water was dipped up and strained and put to my lips. I swallowed a little and revived; but the water was so foul that my stomach rejected it, and I fainted again. Then a little of this water was thrown into my face; and at length I revived sufficiently to go upstairs.

"In the meantime my brother had slipped out and gone down to assist in the landing of the remainder of our company, whom we had left in the boats. When the soldiers discovered that he had disappeared, they at once notified the governor, who had search made for him and found him helping the others ashore. The followers were all brought to the barracks together and

THE BARRACKS IN 'AKKÁ
where the exiles were imprisoned.

lodged on the ground floor. Among them were the women and children, almost dying with hunger and parched with thirst. My brother begged to be permitted to go out for food and water. The soldiers replied: 'You cannot put a foot outside of this room. If you do, we will kill you. Our orders are not to let you leave the barracks under any pretext.' Then he asked permission to send out a servant guarded by soldiers. This was refused.

"The above was related to us by my brother, when he at length returned to our family quarters, in reply to our inquiries as to the occasion of his absence. He had been away for hours, and our hearts had been filled with anxiety for his safety.

"Then came another time of heart-sickening suffering. The mothers who had babes at breast had no milk for them, for lack of food and drink, so the babes could not be pacified or quieted. The larger children were screaming for food and water, and could not sleep or be soothed. The women were fainting.

"Under these conditions, my brother spent the first part of the night in passing about among the distressed people, trying to pacify them, and in appealing to the soldiers not to be so heartless as to allow women and children to suffer so. About midnight he succeeded in getting a message to the governor. We were then sent a little water and some cooked rice; but the latter was so full of grit and smelled so badly that only the strongest stomach could retain it. The water the children drank;

but the rice only the strongest could eat. Later on, some of our people in unpacking their goods found some pieces of the bread which had been brought from Gallipoli, and a little sugar. With these a dish was prepared for the Blessed Perfection, who was very ill. When it was taken to him, he said: 'I command you to take this to the children.' So it was given to them, and they were somewhat quieted.

"The next morning conditions were no better; there was neither water nor food that could be eaten. My brother sent message after message to the governor, appealing in behalf of the women and children. At length he sent us water and some prisoners' bread; but the latter was worse even than the rice—appearing and tasting as though earth had been mixed with the flour. My brother also succeeded in getting permission to send out a servant, guarded by four soldiers, to buy food. But before this permission was given, the governor commanded the presence of my brother and told him that neither he nor any of our people—not even a child—was to leave the prison under any circumstances whatever, and that unless this was promised the servant would not be permitted to go out. Under the circumstances my brother was obliged to give this promise.

"The servant selected was told that if he spoke to a man or woman except in bargaining for supplies, he would be spitted on the swords of the soldiers.

"The servant procured some provisions; yet even

thus we were still badly off for food, for we were all so poor that we could buy but little. So the Blessed Perfection requested that the prison allowance for our support should be commuted for money. The governor consented, and gave to my father the amount allowed our family, and to my brother the amount allowed to the others. Then my father gave his own share and that of our family to my brother for the people, the whole being insufficient for them, saying: 'I will eat bread.' Thereafter, when the supply of provisions was insufficient and he learned of it, he would take only bread and water.

"When we were first brought to the barracks we had no knowledge as to the manner of life to which we were to be consigned. We feared that the Blessed Perfection, my brother, and perhaps others would be placed in dungeons and chained. The only information about it which we could obtain was that our sentence would be read on Friday—our arrival being early in the week. This uncertainty was an additional horror. When the sentence was read to us, we learned that it stated that we were political prisoners, nihilists, murderers, and thieves; that wherever we went, we corrupted the morals of the people; that we had leagued to overthrow the Ottoman Empire; that we could be given no leniency, and that the orders to keep us under bolt and bar must not be broken. It was because of this evil reputation, which had doubtless been given to the government by those who had reasons for desiring our

THE PRISON OF 'AKKA

showing the windows to the room of Bahá'u'lláh, upper right.

destruction, and not from any want of humanity on the part of our jailors, who later became very kind and friendly to us, that we were subjected to such stern treatment and were given no more latitude or aid.

"The season was summer (1868) and the temperature very high. All our people were huddled together on the damp earth floor of the barracks; with little water to drink, and that very bad, with no water with which to bathe, and scarcely enough for washing their faces. Typhoid fever and dysentery broke out among them. Every one in our company fell sick excepting my brother, my mother, an aunt, and two others of the believers.[33] We were not allowed a physician; we could not procure medicine. My brother had in his baggage some quinine and bismuth. With these two drugs and his nursing, he brought us all through with the exception of four, who died.[34] These were two months of such awful horror as words cannot picture. Imagine it, if you can. Some seventy men, women, and children[35] packed together, hot summer weather, no proper food, bad water, the most offensive odors from purging and excretions, and a general attack of the terrible diseases of dysentery and typhoid.

"There was no one with strength to be of any general service but my brother. He washed the patients, fed them, nursed them, watched with them. He took no rest. When at length he had brought the rest of us—the four who died excepted—through the crisis and we were out of danger, he was utterly exhausted and fell sick himself, as did also my mother and the three others who had theretofore been well. The others soon recovered, but 'Abbás Effendi was taken with dysentery, and long remained in a dangerous condition. By his heroic exertions he had won the regard of one of the officers, and when this man saw my brother in this state he went to the governor and pleaded that 'Abbás Effendi might have a physician. This was permitted, and under the care of the physician my brother recovered.

"For long after our departure from Adrianople none of the friends and followers of the Blessed Perfection in Persia knew our whereabouts. We were not permitted to send any letters. Great efforts were made to find us, and our friends finally traced us to 'Akká; but this whole city was then practically a prison from which strangers were carefully excluded, and they found it impossible to get into communication with us, or even to pass the city gate.

"There was a Persian follower of the Báb* who some time before, having failed in his business at home, had emigrated to 'Akká.[36] He had not dared to disclose his faith, and no one suspected it. The servant who marketed for us happened one day, as he went about the bazaar to come to this man's shop; and though he was not allowed to speak with him, he seems to have known intuitively that he was a friend. So thereafter he made most of his purchases of provisions at his shop.

---

*Mírzá 'Abdu'l-Ahad, who had been asked by 'Abdu'l-Bahá to settle in 'Akká prior to Bahá'u'lláh's exile to that city. — ED.

Some of the Persian believers who had come to 'Akká, but who had been unable to enter the city, effected communication with this man and arranged with him to send a note to the Blessed Perfection. This the shopkeeper accomplished by concealing the note among some vegetables and giving them to the servant with such a look that the latter understood and afterwards searched for it. The note begged the Blessed Perfection to send out some word; but this seemed to be beyond our power.

"The physician who visited my brother, on seeing our condition, had so much sympathy with our distress, and became so fond of 'Abbás Effendi, that he asked him if there was not something which he could do for us. My brother begged him to take a message to the believers who were waiting to hear from the Blessed Perfection. He undertook to do so, and carried a tablet away in the lining of his hat. For two years this physician conveyed tablets and messages to and fro for us in this way.

"After this first message had been transmitted from the Blessed Perfection, many believers came here from Persia and remained in the neighbourhood with the hope of effecting some communication with him, or at least of getting a glimpse of him. They would go to some prominent point where they could be seen from his window. Some of us, seeing them, would call my brother's attention to them, whereupon he would inform the Blessed Perfection and follow him to the window and wave his handkerchief.

86

"We were imprisoned in the barracks, without any substantial change in our manner of life, for two years. During this time none of us left the prison—not even my brother or any of the children. The Blessed Perfection passed his time in his room, writing tablets, or rather dictating them to my younger brother, who was a rapid penman. 'Abbás Effendi would copy them and send them out by the physician.

"It was usual to carry on this work during the evening. One evening towards the end of the second year, my younger brother came, as was his habit, to write for his father. But as he was not very well, and as some others of the family were also ill, the Blessed Perfection told him to go and come later. So he went up to the flat roof of the barracks, where we were accustomed to walk, and which was our only recourse for fresh air and exercise. He was walking up and down, repeating tablets and gazing at the sky, when he stumbled, lost his balance, and fell through the opening to which the ladder from below led up. The room into which he fell had a lofty ceiling; it was the living-room of the family. No one was in the room at the time, but, hearing his cries, some of the family rushed in and found him lying in a heap on the floor with the blood pouring from his mouth. The Blessed Perfection, hearing the commotion, opened the door of his room and looked out. When he saw his son he turned back and reentered his room, saying: 'Mihdí has gone!'

"We took him up and laid him on his mat. He was

MÍRZÁ MIHDÍ, THE PUREST BRANCH

perfectly conscious. Later the Blessed Perfection came and remained with him. The physician was sent for; he said that there was no hope.

"My brother lived for about thirty hours. When he was about to pass away the Blessed Perfection said to him: 'What do you desire? Do you wish to live, or do you prefer to die? Tell me what you most wish for.' My brother replied: 'I don't care to live. I have but one wish. I want the believers to be admitted to see their Lord. If you will promise me this, it is all I ask.' The Blessed Perfection told him that it would be as he desired.

"So, after much patient suffering, my brother's gentle spirit took its flight. As we could not leave the barracks, we could not bury our dead; nor had we the consolation of feeling that we could provide for him through others the grateful final tribute of a proper and fitting burial, as we had no means wherewith even to purchase a coffin. After some consideration and con- sultation among ourselves, finding that we had nothing to dispose of, and at a loss how to proceed, we told our Lord* of the sad situation. He replied that there was a rug in his room which we could sell. At first we de- murred, for in taking his rug we took the only comfort he had; but he insisted and we sold it. A coffin was then procured, and the remains of my deceased brother

*Bahá'u'lláh. — M.H.P.

89

placed in it. It was carried out by our jailors, and we did not even know whither it was taken.*

"The death of this youngest and favorite child—of a very gentle and sweet disposition—nearly broke his mother's heart. We feared for her reason. When the Blessed Perfection was told of the condition of his wife, he went to her and said: 'Your son has been taken by God that His people might be freed. His life was the ransom, and you should rejoice that you had a son so dear to give to the cause of God.' When our mother heard these words she seemed to rally,—knelt, and kissed the Blessed Perfection's hands, and thanked him for what he had said. After that she did not shed a tear.[37]

"I should perhaps here say a word about our relations, in the family, to the Blessed Perfection. After his declaration we all regarded him as one far above us, and tacitly gave him a corresponding position in our demeanor towards him. He was never called upon to consider, or take part in, any worldly matters. We felt no claim upon him because of family relationship—no more than that of his other followers. When we had but two rooms for all, one was set apart for him. The best of everything was always given to him. He would take it and then return it to us and do without. He slept upon

---

*It was later ascertained that the remains of Mírzá Mihdí, the Purest Branch, had been interred in the cemetery next to the shrine of Nabí Sálih, in 'Akká. Some fifty years later, they were transferred to the Bahá'í Monument Gardens on Mt. Carmel.—ED.

the floor because his people had no beds, although he would have been furnished one had he wished it.

"Some time after the death of his son, the Blessed Perfection (who, as I have said, usually never attended to affairs, these being all left to my brother) expressed a wish to have an interview with the governor. Meanwhile my brother's dying prayer, that the believers might be permitted to visit their Lord, having been overheard by a soldier who was present at the time and by him repeated to the officer in charge, had come to the ears of the governor. Very possibly it had touched him and now influenced him to accede to the Blessed Perfection's request for an interview; at all events the request was granted, and the Blessed Perfection met the governor in council with his officers. He then addressed them on the subject of his separation from his followers and of their great sorrow and distress occasioned by it, reminding them of his deceased son's dying petition, and speaking with such eloquence and power that the governor was moved to grant his appeal.

"We were, in consequence, removed from the barracks and given a comfortable house with three rooms and a court.* Our people, and also our family, were permitted to go at large in the city, and whoever wished could visit us; but my father was required to remain within the house."[38]

Just here I wish to interrupt the narrative in order to

*The house of 'Údí Khammár. — ED.

THE HOUSE OF 'ABBÚD,

front, showing the House of 'Údí Khammár, directly behind, where the exiles lived.

call attention to what seems to me a very remarkable fact. Notwithstanding this interminable catalogue of the extreme and almost incredible sufferings and privations which this heroic band of men and women have endured—more terrible than many martyrdoms—there is not a trace of resentment or bitterness to be observed amongst them. One would suppose that they were the most fortunate of the people among whom they live, as, indeed, they do certainly consider themselves, in that they have always been permitted to live near their beloved Lord, beside which they count their sufferings as nothing. They well know that those having their own motives for maligning them have persistently misled the sultan's advisers as to their real character and purposes; and that their implacable enemies have been, not the authorities of the state, but those allied to them both by nationality and close ties of family relationship. Except as these have interfered and caused prejudice and trouble, they consider their treatment by the government humane and even kind. Moreover, they recognise the fact that the deplorable attack upon the life of the Shah of Persia, while in no sense their fault, has been inevitably their misfortune, rationally explaining much of the suspicion and harsh treatment to which they have been subjected.

When all is fairly considered, it must be acknowledged that the sultan is fair and liberal in the treatment of religious opinions, provided that these opinions are not used as a shield for hostile political purposes and intrigues. Men of many various faiths dwell together in peace, harmony, and contentment in all parts of his dominions.

We should beware, moreover, of hasty criticism, remembering how difficult it is for a sovereign to penetrate to the truth of such matters, easily obscured by the perversions of hostile interests which have his ear; and we may hope that the patient resignation and good lives of 'Abbás Effendi and his little band of followers at 'Akká may at length convince his Majesty that, as is, indeed, the fact, he has not in his dominions more loyal subjects or more useful citizens.*

*'Abdu'l-Bahá was eventually freed in 1908, after the Young Turk Revolution. — ED.

THE MOSQUE OF 'AKKÁ

CHAPTER V

THE STORY OF HIS LIFE (*Concluded*)

'AKKÁ

" A MONG THOSE who went with us from Adrianople
to 'Akká were three men who were followers of
Ṣubḥ-i Azal, and also one of Ṣubḥ-i Azal's wives who,
having quarreled with him, asked permission to accompany us.* During the two years of close confinement
these four lived peaceably with the followers of the
Blessed Perfection, the woman in his family.[39] As soon
as our company was released from the barracks, they
began to make mischief. They slandered the believers
to the people of 'Akká, saying that we would make
trouble at the first opportunity, and other things of like
nature. The men were relatives of the woman, and she
asked permission to live with them. So they took up
quarters together in another part of the town from that
in which we lived.

*The Azalís intended are apparently Sayyid Muḥammad-i
Iṣfahání, Áqá Ján-i Kaj-Kuláh, and Mírzá Riḍá-Qulíy-i Tafrishí.
Azal's wife was Badrí-Ján (Badr-i Jahán). — ED.

"After this their hostility became more aggressive and open. They declared that they were imprisoned by mistake, being enemies of the Blessed Perfection; threatened to kill the Blessed Perfection and my brother, if there should be an opportunity; and carried on various intrigues against them, as the forging of letters purporting to come from the Blessed Perfection and saying evil things of the sultan and the governor, which they took to the officials. At length they were so successful in inviting trouble that a threat came from Constantinople of again transporting and separating us.

"Two of the believers[40] thought that they would settle the matter themselves, without taking counsel with the Blessed Perfection or my brother. They reasoned that if they should take such counsel, they would be forbidden to execute their plans, and, having been forbidden, they could not disobey. 'We will,' they said, 'do a wicked deed; but we will stop the evil doings of these people even if we are cursed for it. We will save our Lord though at the risk of our own souls.' They persuaded another of the believers to join them and the three proceeded to the house of the Azalís. Their intention was to demand of them a promise to stop their mischief, under threat of death; but they did not have the opportunity to get so far as that. Having called the Azalís out they asked them whether they intended to kill the Blessed Perfection and the Master; whereupon the Azalís attacked them fiercely with clubs and sticks. A general fight followed in which two Azalís and one Bahá'í were killed.[41]

"In consequence of this affair (which occurred very soon after our release from the barracks) my brother was arrested and put in chains in the dungeon, on the assertion by the surviving Azalí and the woman with him that he and the Blessed Perfection had instigated the trouble. Then followed another period of misery. The Blessed Perfection was brought before the court and gave testimony in behalf of himself and my brother. 'Abbás Effendi was speedily released from prison, but remained under suspicion, and the matter was not determined for many months, during which we lived in terrible suspense and anxiety. But at length the court was satisfied that the charges were baseless, and they were withdrawn.*

"The Blessed Perfection then excommunicated the two Bahá'ís who were in the fight and survived it: they

---

*Professor Browne (A *Traveller's Narrative*, p. 370) quotes Laurence Oliphant as saying that Bahá'u'lláh, on being brought before the court on this occasion, and being asked who and what he was, replied: "I will begin by telling you who I am not. I am not a camel-driver," — an allusion to the prophet Muḥammad, — "nor am I the son of a carpenter," — an allusion to Christ. "This is as much as I can tell you today. If you will now let me retire, I will tell you tomorrow who I am." "Upon this promise," continues Mr. Oliphant, "he was let go; but the morrow never came. With an enormous bribe he had in the interval purchased an exemption from all further attendance at court."

I called 'Abbás Effendi's attention to this statement, and asked him if there was any truth in it. "There is none whatever," he replied. "You can see for yourself that Bahá'u'lláh could not have made those remarks. This being a Turkish government, the officials are all Muhammadans. There are also a very large number of Christians here. All Muhammadans and Christians would have understood the allusions; and such remarks being disrespectful to

never again had speech with him. He soon after began a series of tablets on the sin of murder; declaring that no one, whosoever he might be, who would take the life of his brother, could be a Bahá'í.

"The woman and the surviving Azalí were sent to Constantinople.[42]

"These, so far as I have ever heard, were the only Azalís who have been killed by Bahá'ís.

"After our liberation from the barracks and the termination of this affair, my brother was able to mingle freely with the people of 'Akká, and he at once began to establish friendly relations with them. As illustrating the manner in which he gradually won their good-will,

---

Muhammad and Christ, and the Blessed Perfection being a prisoner accused of endeavoring to subvert religious faith, they would have cut him in pieces — he could never have left the courtroom.

"What the Blessed Perfection actually said in his own behalf was in substance this:

" 'I am innocent of any knowledge of this matter. How could I, who teach love and pity for every creature — who have given my life and that of my family to demonstrate that this is true religion — instigate this thing?

" 'You are trying to fasten upon me a guilt of which I am innocent; but I am ready to die. If you wish to execute me, I will sign any paper which you may prepare consenting to my execution; but I declare to you that I am innocent of this accusation.'

"The trial of these men lasted six months; during all this time the effort was being made to fasten the guilt upon the Blessed Perfection. Moreover, this trial was before a judge and jury. Is it likely that under these circumstances he could have bribed both a judge and a jury, who were, besides, to begin with, not too well disposed towards him? The effort would have been futile had he attempted it. He did not, nor would he have done so under any circumstances."
—M.H.P.

an incident occurs to me which I will relate. The believers needed fuel, but the people would not sell it to them. They regarded us as heretics and thought there was merit for them in harshness and unkindness towards us. 'Abbás Effendi obtained permission to send out of the city for charcoal, and a camel-load was brought back. The driver was stopped by a Christian merchant. 'This is better charcoal than I can get,' he said, and without more ceremony took it for himself — nor would he return the money paid for it.

"This was reported to my brother. He went to the merchant's shop and stood in the door. He was not noticed. Then he entered and sat down by the door. The merchant continuing to transact his business with those who came and paying him no attention, he waited in silence for three hours. At length, when the others had left and no more came, the merchant said to him: 'Are you one of those prisoners here?' 'Abbás Effendi assenting, he continued: 'What have you done that you are imprisoned?'

" 'Since you ask me,' replied 'Abbás Effendi, 'I will tell you. We have done nothing. We are persecuted as Christ was persecuted.'

" 'What do you know of Christ?' said the merchant.

"My brother replied in such a manner that the merchant perceived that he was not ignorant of Christ and the Christian Bible. He then began to question him about the Bible and was interested in his replies, as my brother gave him explanations which he had never before heard.

THE GREATEST HOLY LEAF WITH SHOGHI EFFENDI

"Next he invited my brother to a seat beside him and continued the conversation for two hours. At its conclusion he seemed much pleased, and said: 'The coal is gone, — I cannot return you that, but here is the money.' He then escorted my brother to the door and down into the street, treating him with the greatest respect. Since that time he and 'Abbás Effendi have been fast friends, and the two families also.

"Yet the prejudices and animosities of the people against us were so deep-rooted that much time and patience have been required to remove them. You have already been told, I think, of the Afghan who persisted in his enmity for twenty-four years, but was finally softened by my brother's kindnesses. So it has been with many. But in time his love for others has won all hearts. People have commonly said of him: 'What does he do to his enemies that he makes them his friends?'

"The governor, the magistrates, the officers of the army, first learned to respect him, and then to love him. Nearly every one in the city loves him, — Muslim and Christian, rich and poor.

"Yet perhaps there is one exception — I know of no other — of which I will now speak.

"The Blessed Perfection indicated in many ways that 'Abbás Effendi was to be his successor. Many years before his death he declared this in his *Book of Laws* [the Kitáb-i Aqdas]. He has referred to 'Abbás Effendi as 'The Center of my Covenant,' 'The Greatest Branch,' 'The Branch from the Ancient Root,' 'The Mystery of the Greatest God.' He conferred upon him the designation of 'His Highness the Master,' and usually so addressed him and spoke of him; and he required all his family to treat him with marked deference. He also left a testament in which he reiterated his will in this respect.

"Nevertheless, after the death of the Blessed Perfection, 'Abbás Effendi's assumption of this position was resented by our half brother, Mírzá Muḥammad-'Alí. For a time he endeavored to stir up dissensions among the Bahá'ís. Failing in this, he sought to injure my brother personally. At this time, as had been the case for more than twenty years, my brother was permitted to go at his pleasure beyond the walls of 'Akká, and had the freedom of the surrounding country. I then myself resided in Haifa, and he as well as the other members of his family were in the habit of going there frequently, a change which was of much benefit to their health, since 'Akká is a small, crowded, and, in some seasons, unhealthy city. Muḥammad-'Alí proceeded to make false charges of various sorts against 'Abbás Effendi to the Turkish government. One of these was this:

"The Blessed Perfection before his death gave 'Abbás Effendi the charge to build, on a site which he had selected on the side of Mt. Carmel above Haifa, a building which should be the permanent resting-place of the remains of the Báb, himself, and my brother, and also contain a hall for meeting and worship.* This

---

*Both 'Abdu'l-Bahá and Shoghi Effendi, the subsequent Guardian of the Bahá'í Faith, have made it clear that the interment of the remains of the Master in the Shrine of the Báb is to be only tem-

TWO WOMEN OF THE HOUSEHOLD
Ḍíyá'íyyih Khánum (l.) and unknown.

building was in process of erection at the time I speak of—it is not yet completed—and Muḥammad-'Alí represented to the authorities that it was intended as a fort, in which 'Abbás Effendi and his followers intended to entrench themselves, defy the government, and endeavor to gain possession of this part of Syria.

"Other equally baseless charges were fabricated and reiterated until the goverment, as on previous occasions, became weary of the annoyance and issued a *firman* decreeing that the original order, by which the Blessed Perfection and his family were confined within the walls of 'Akká, should be again put in force.

"This was about two years ago. Since that time my brother has been assured that on his application in behalf of himself alone, his strict confinement would be again remitted. He refuses, however, to make this application.* This is because he is much more grieved by his brother's alienation from himself than by his own loss of freedom. He regards harboring hatred against another as the greatest evil which can befall a man, and

---

porary. Eventually, they must be removed to a separate Shrine to be built in an appropriate location at the World Center of the Faith. — ED.

*Further, in the fall of 1902, a number of American friends of 'Abbás Effendi formed the plan of visiting the court of the Shah of Persia and securing his cooperation in an application to the Sultan of Turkey for the release of 'Abbás Effendi. They came to Europe for this purpose, and from Paris telegraphed to 'Abbás Effendi asking his assent to the project. He replied, requesting that the undertaking should be abandoned. — M.H.P.

he is determined to rescue his brother from this, if possible, at whatever cost to himself. He knows that his own liberation would cause Muḥammad-'Alí's hatred to increase, and probably render a reconciliation impossible; but he hopes that, if the situation remains as it is, he may in time be able to soften his brother's heart and regain his love.*

"My father's imprisonment in his house continued for nine years after our release from the barracks.† His followers from abroad now had free access to him, and our life was in most respects comparatively comfortable. After this time the governor gave the Blessed Perfection the freedom of the city, and of the country in the vicinity of 'Akká. His friends now urged him to reside in the country, believing that his health would be benefited by the change.⁴³ He at first refused, but at

---

*As this book is about to go to press, I am informed of an event which has caused great rejoicing in the Bahá'í world. Besides Muḥammad-'Alí, 'Abbás Effendi has another half brother (full brother to the former), by the name Badí'u'lláh. Badí'u'lláh has always maintained friendly relations with 'Abbás Effendi and his family, but has sided with Muḥammad-'Alí in his protest against recognizing 'Abbás Effendi as the head of the church. He has now repented of his apostasy, and in a lengthy manifesto, a copy of which I have seen, announces his adherence to 'Abbás Effendi as the true "Center of the Covenant." — M.H.P.

Mírzá Badí'u'lláh's repentance was, however, short-lived. He eventually abandoned 'Abdu'l-Bahá and returned to the fold of the Covenant-breakers. — ED.

†Bahá'u'lláh's stay in the House of 'Abbúd was seven years. The nine years was from the time of the arrival of the prisoners in 'Akká. — ED.

length yielded to persuasion and transferred his
residence to a house without the city.* Here he passed
a quiet and peaceful life until his death at the age of
seventy-five, in the year 1892. His chief occupation, as
it had been at all times since his return from his sojourn
of two years alone in the mountains near Baghdad, was
the writing of sacred books and tablets.

*Professor Browne visited Bahá'u'lláh there in 1890, and his
graphic description of his first interview with him is so effective and
interesting that I will quote it. "I . . . was conducted," he says,
"through passages and rooms at which I scarcely had time to glance
to a spacious hall, paved, so far as I remember (for my mind was
occupied with other thoughts) with a mosaic of marble. Before a
curtain suspended from the wall of this great ante-chamber my con-
ductor paused for a moment while I removed my shoes. Then, with
a quick movement of the hand, he withdrew, and, as I passed,
replaced the curtain; and I found myself in a large apartment, along
the upper end of which ran a low divan, while on the side opposite
the door were placed two or three chairs. Though I dimly suspected
whither I was going and whom I was to behold (for no distinct in-
timation had been given to me), a second or two elapsed ere, with a
throb of wonder and awe, I became definitely conscious that the
room was not untenanted. In the corner where the divan met the
wall sat a wondrous and venerable figure, crowned with a felt head-
dress of the kind called *táj* by dervishes (but of unusual height and
make), round the base of which was wound a small white turban.
The face of him on whom I gazed I can never forget, though I cannot describe it. Those piercing eyes seemed to read one's very soul;
power and authority sat on that ample brow; while the deep lines on
the forehead and face implied an age which the jet-black hair and
beard flowing down in indistinguishable luxuriance almost to the
waist seemed to belie. No need to ask in whose presence I stood, as
I bowed myself before one who is the object of a devotion and love
which kings might envy and emperors sigh for in vain!
"A mild dignified voice bade me be seated, and then continued: —
'Praise be to God that thou hast attained! . . . Thou hast come to see

"'Abbás Effendi continued to live in 'Akká. He frequently visited the Blessed Perfection, and generally came out on foot. The walk was long, and in summer the sun very oppressive. It was his habit, if overcome with heat or fatigue, to lie down on the ground, rest his head on a stone, and sleep. The Blessed Perfection remonstrated with him about this, saying that he should use a horse. My brother replied, 'How can I come to my Lord riding? I must show that I am the humblest of all the people. When Christ went out he walked, and slept in the fields. Who am I, that in visiting my Lord I should go as greater than Christ?'

"In his early life my brother was much disinclined to

---

a prisoner and an exile. . . . We desire but the good of the world and the happiness of the nations; yet they deem us a stirrer up of strife and sedition worthy of bondage and banishment. . . . That all nations should become one in faith and all men as brothers; that the bonds of affection and unity between the sons of men should be strengthened; that diversity of religion should cease, and differences of race be annulled — what harm is there in this? . . . Yet so it shall be; these fruitless strifes, these ruinous wars shall pass away, and the "Most Great Peace" shall come. . . . Do not you in Europe need this also? Is not this that which Christ foretold? . . . Yet do we see your kings and rulers lavishing their treasures more freely on means for the destruction of the human race than on that which would conduce to the happiness of mankind . . . These strifes and this bloodshed and discord must cease, and all men be as one kindred and one family. . . . Let not a man glory in this, that he loves his country; let him rather glory in this, that he loves his kind. . . . '

"Such, so far as I can recall them, were the words which, besides many others, I heard from Behá. Let those who read them consider well with themselves whether such doctrines merit death and bonds, and whether the world is more likely to gain or lose by their diffusion." — M.H.P.

marry. It is a Persian custom, when two cousins, a boy and girl, are born about the same time, to promise them in marriage to each other in their infancy. My brother was promised in this way to a cousin, and while we lived in Baghdad we thought that the time had come for the marriage. He, however, thought differently; and when our mother desired to send for the girl, he positively refused to permit it to be done. 'Why should I marry?' he asked; 'Are there not enough to suffer now, that we should propose to bring others to share our lot?'[44]

"After our release from the two-years' confinement in the barracks here, my mother and myself were both very desirous that my brother should marry, and we began to look about for a girl whom we would approve. Our choice finally fell upon the daughter of a believer living in Syria, who was said to be very beautiful and amiable, and in every way a suitable match. Without consulting my brother, since we wished to place him in a position where he could not refuse our oft-repeated appeals to give us a daughter and a sister, I invited her to visit us. The invitation was accepted, and she set out with her brother. After a hard and wearisome journey, they reached Haifa and were taken to the house of one of my uncles there.

"We commenced quietly to make preparations for the marriage, without making known to my brother the arrival of the girl. However, many of the believers knew of it and of our intentions, and were so delighted that 'their Master' (as they always called him) was to take a wife, thus giving them the hope that he might have a son to succeed him in fostering the faith until it should become established, that their pleasure shone in their faces. My brother saw that there was something unusual afoot, and the thought occurred to him, since the subject had been so much urged upon him, 'Now perhaps they are getting me a wife.' So he hastened home to us and demanded with considerable energy, 'What is this—what are all the people smiling about? Is it possible that you are again planning to get me a wife? If you are, you may as well give it up, for I will not marry.' We tried to plead and reason with him, but he would not hear us. Finally we said, 'What, then, is to be done? She is at Haifa—she has come with her brother—what can we do?'* Then he hesitated, looked serious, and finally said: 'Well, if you have brought her here, she belongs to me, and I will give her in marriage to some one who will be better suited to make her happy than I.'

"She remained at Haifa for some time, until at length my brother brought about her marriage to a husband of his own selection. The marriage has resulted satisfactorily to all parties.

"The Báb, during his life, had a certain follower who was specially devoted to him. On one occasion he

---

*To have returned the girl to her home unmarried, under these circumstances, would have brought dishonor on her and her family. — ED.

visited this man in his home. His host said to him that
his visit filled him with the greatest happiness of his
life; but that he had one sorrow of which he wished to
speak. He had been married ten years, and was
childless. He begged the Báb to pray for a child for
him, and this the Báb promised.[45]

"Nine months later a daughter* was born to this
follower. When this daughter grew up she was very
sweet and very amiable. She had been promised in her
infancy to a cousin; and her cousin, in due time, was
very desirous for the marriage. Having been permitted
to see her, from that day on he seemed to think of
nothing but the time when she should be his wife. He
urged on the marriage, provided the house, and made
all the usual preparations. On the day set, the bride was
brought to the bridegroom's house, which, according to
Persian custom, completed the civil marriage. Then, to
every one's amazement and consternation, the bridegroom refused to see the bride. To the demands of the
relatives as to why he had changed his mind within an
hour his only reply was, 'I do not know. I cannot explain and have nothing to tell. All I know is that I
cannot see her.'

"Six months later the young man died.

"The girl remained in her husband's house until his
death; but she never saw him after entering it.[46]

"She felt much humiliated, and resolved that she

*Fátimih, later named Munírih Khánum by Bahá'u'lláh. — ED.

MUNÍRIH KHÁNUM, THE HOLY MOTHER
The wife of 'Abdu'l-Bahá.

THE GREATEST HOLY LEAF (right) WITH
MUNÍRIH KHÁNUM

would never again marry. She and her family were very earnest believers; and after this occurrence she begged her father and mother to send her to be a servant in the household of the Blessed Perfection. Because of her disappointment her parents did not wish to refuse her; and her mother wrote for permission to visit the family of the Blessed Perfection with her daughter. Permission was granted and they came to Haifa. The Blessed Perfection asked my brother to bring them; but, not finding it convenient to go himself, he gave the commission to some one else to execute. Mother and daughter came to our house, and, having seen the Blessed Perfection, asked to see the Master. At that moment my brother entered and conversed briefly with the ladies, seeming, however, unusually interested for him.

"The ladies returned to Haifa and remained there,[47] coming back and forth occasionally to visit us. My mother and I, seeing that my brother was noticing the young woman, hoped that he might marry her; but, remembering our experience, we did not dare to suggest it. About six months later the Blessed Perfection called my brother to his room and asked him if he would not take this young woman for his wife. My brother consented.

"In deciding to marry, my brother undoubtedly sacrificed his own preference for a single life to the wishes of the rest of the family, and especially of the Blessed Perfection. The latter had suggested to him that, as his example would influence all believers, it would be well if it illustrated the best and highest condition of life for men, which was the married state. Yet, in coming to this decision, I think that our Master was much influenced by the warm regard and affection which he undoubtedly felt for the woman whom he was asked to marry.

"Then there was much rejoicing. All the believers looked forward to the marriage with delight. But time went on and yet it was not concluded. The real reason, which we did not care to mention publicly, was that we had no suitable room to give my brother in the house, and were not willing to lose him from our home, where his presence was so essential to our happiness.

"Finally, I went to the wife of our landlord and told her of our perplexity. She consulted her husband, and he, a good-natured man, said that he could remove the difficulty. He owned the adjoining house; and he cut a door to connect the courts of the two houses, and gave us a room, completely furnished, in the other house.

"The way was thus made plain for the marriage, and it was duly solemnized soon after.

"The occasion of the wedding had one peculiar feature so characteristic of my brother that I will mention it. Our marriage service is very simple, consisting of the reading of a tablet and the exchange of promises by the contracting parties.[48] It is usually followed by feasting and the entertainment of friends until late at night.

COURTYARD IN THE HOUSE OF 'ABBÚD

"Our Master had made, personally and with great care, all the preparations for receiving and entertaining the guests. The ceremony was performed by the Blessed Perfection about two P.M. My brother then quietly withdrew without speaking to any one, and did not return until after the guests had dispersed.

"It was not from want of consideration for the solemnity of the occasion or for his bride that he did this, for the tender affection which he has always shown for her disproves this; or for his guests, for his minute attention to the arrangements for their pleasure disproves this also. But it was his habit to spend this part of the day and the evening in visiting the poor and sick and explaining the Qur'án, he being frequently thus occupied until a late hour. He never permitted his own affairs to interfere with the discharge of these duties, and was unwilling to neglect them even on this occasion.[49]

"My brother's marriage has proved exceedingly happy and harmonious. Several months ago my sister [-in-law] took two of her daughters to Beirut on account of their health, and this has been her first separation from her husband for any length of time. Since a short time after her departure a question repeated by my brother the first thing every morning to his daughter, who is his constant attendant, is, 'Ruha, when do you think your mother will come back?'

"Eight children have been born to them, of whom four are living. Their family now consists of two unmar-

Women of the Holy Household. Standing (l. to r.): Unknown, Unknown, Unknown, Julia Culver, Emogene Hoagg, Maryam, Unknown, Zaynat (wife of Dr. Zia Bagdadi), Mihranghíz, Unknown. Seated: Surayá, Munírih Khánum (wife of 'Abdu'l-Bahá), Bahíyyih Khánum (the Greatest Holy Leaf), and (the daughters of 'Abdu'l-Bahá) Díyá'íyyih Khánum, Túbá Khánum, and Rúhá Khánum. Children seated on the carpet: Ḥasan, Zahrá, Riyál, Unknown, Parvín (daughter of Dr. Bagdadi), Fu'ád.

ried daughters, two married daughters with their families, and myself.*

"Many influences, and those of the very strongest character, have been brought to induce my brother to take a second wife—a practice which the Blessed Perfection did not in terms forbid, but advised against.† The believers have urged it strongly for several reasons. Very many of them wish to take a second wife themselves, but feel constrained from doing so by the Master's example. In Persia, except among believers, polygamy is a universal custom, and the restriction to one wife, which all believers feel and respect, seems very severe. Then there is a general wish that the Master might have a son to succeed him. Other arguments have been advanced; and the pressure brought to bear upon him has been, and still is, very great—greater than you can easily imagine.

"The general advice of the Blessed Perfection against a second marriage would in itself have had the effect with my brother of a command and have settled the question; but as regards him it was withdrawn by our Lord before his death. He said to 'Abbás Effendi that he rather wished to lead the believers gradually to

---

*The married daughters: Díyá'íyyih Khánum (the mother of Shoghi Effendi) and Túbá Khánum; the unmarried daughters: Rúhá Khánum and Munavvar Khánum. — ED.

†The text of the Kitáb-i Aqdas forbids more than two wives, but conditions bigamy upon justice. Since justice is impossible in such a circumstance, as 'Abdu'l-Bahá later explained, monogamy alone is permissible for Bahá'ís. — ED.

monogamy than to force them to adopt it, which they felt bound to do by reason of the Master's example; that therefore, and since it was much desired by all that the Master should have a son, he withdrew even the advice in his case, and desired him to consider himself free to follow his own desires and inclination.

"To this the Master replied that his own wishes and feelings were against a second marriage, though, if the Blessed Perfection should command it, he would obey. This, however, the Blessed Perfection never did.

"To all other appeals his reply has always been a firm refusal. He thinks that if it had been God's will that he should leave a son, the two who had been born to him would not have been taken away.[50] He believes that the best and highest condition of life for a man is marriage to one wife, and that it is his duty to set that example to the world."

'ABDU'L-BAHÁ

CHAPTER VI

CHARACTERISTICS AND INCIDENTS

I SHALL now collect some of my own observations with regard to 'Abbás Effendi, and a number of incidents of his life related to me by others, which throw light upon and illustrate his character, but which I am not able to make a part of any consecutive narrative.* I am aware that in doing this I am disregarding literary symmetry; but as my only object in preparing this book is to give those who read it as much information as possible about him and his teachings, I do not wish to omit any material which may contribute to this end.

The characteristic of 'Abbás Effendi, regarded as a religious leader, which is at once the most striking, the most attractive, and the most impressive, is his generous and tolerant liberality. It is disappointing to find that narrowness and intolerance have already

---

*Many of the stories and reports that are related in this chapter cannot be confirmed by other sources. Since the author states clearly here that these vignettes were "related to me by others," they cannot be regarded as eyewitness accounts or as absolutely accurate statements of what took place. — ED.

shown themselves in the teachings of some of his followers—a perversion and degradation of true religion which is seen to be an almost inevitable tendency of human nature in all ages of the world, and which most religions have suffered in the hands of their adherents. The chief glory of Bahaism is that its true spirit, as exemplified in its Great Apostle, is utterly free from it.

I shall state at length his attitude in this respect in a subsequent chapter,* here merely mentioning two incidents illustrating it, which were related to me in 'Akká.

One was that of a gentleman who wrote to 'Abbás Effendi to this effect: That he recognised him as a man of great spiritual force, and one who, in urging upon men the observance of the Law of Love, was doing much in the service of humanity; that he desired to work with him and for him; but that also he ('Abbás Effendi) had said some things with which he did not agree, and that he himself had some spiritual light, which he did not wish to surrender.

'Abbás Effendi replied that he welcomed him as a coworker; that he asked him to give up nothing; that he approved of his continuing to adhere to any religious faith with which he might be associated, and that the one thing necessary was to love God above all things and seek Him.

*The chapter referred to here has not been included in this reprint. — ED.

The other case was that of a lady who was visiting 'Abbás Effendi in 'Akká. She had accepted him as her religious teacher, and desired to assist in spreading his teachings. When about to return to her home, she told him that her associations were all in the orthodox Christian Church, and that her friends would be repelled by the idea of a new religion. He advised her to return as a Christian, to remain in the Christian Church, and to teach what she had learned as the true teaching of Christ.*

'Abbás Effendi has another characteristic as a religious leader which seems to me to be, especially at this time, remarkably refreshing and reassuring—he makes no claim to being a "healer" or to the performance of "miracles." Whether or not he possesses such powers I would not undertake to say; but he certainly regards physical health as of too little importance in comparison with spiritual welfare to merit primary attention. The only real sickness which he recognises is sickness of the soul. The one and exclusive object which he has in view is the spiritual elevation of

*These stories illustrate 'Abdu'l-Bahá's tactful approach to seekers after truth and his emphasis on the Bahá'í principle of the fundamental unity of all religions. It was only gradually that the independent nature of the Bahá'í Faith emerged and became generally recognized. It was the Guardian of the Bahá'í Faith, Shoghi Effendi, who established the principle that Bahá'ís, while associating in complete friendship with followers of other religions, could not remain members of Christian churches, certain of whose teachings are not in accord with those of Bahá'u'lláh. — ED.

'ABDU'L-BAHÁ
walking in the garden near his house in Haifa.

humanity — an all-sufficient end in itself, which does not require for its justification any physical gain.*

Yet, in point of fact, he says there is a physical gain in attaining spiritual health; for the normal effect of this is to promote recovery from bodily disease; and still more, in those cases where the latter is not removed by spiritual regeneration, the spirit which has experienced this change *does not feel* physical pain, and looks upon the sufferings of its body with the same indifference with which the ordinary man regards suffering in the body of another.† The body is, therefore, sometimes restored, and pain is overcome by spiritual force; but these occurrences are properly regarded as unimportant incidents in the attainment of spiritual well-being.

Further, 'Abbás Effendi is very careful not to countenance any interpretation of his acts by his followers which could lead to the imputation to him of miraculous powers. The assertion of such powers for himself or for his predecessors would, he says, stand in the way of

*The author was not always a reliable reporter of 'Abdu'l-Bahá's teachings. His understanding of the Bahá'í Faith was often incomplete or incorrect and colored by his own Buddhist philosophy. (See "Familiar 'Akká Voices," the foreword to this revised edition, pp. xix–xxii.) Therefore, the reader is cautioned not to rely upon this chapter as an authoritative statement of 'Abdu'l-Bahá's views on healing, disease, etc. Such statements should rather be sought in the published writings of 'Abdu'l-Bahá himself. — ED.

†This statement attributed to 'Abdu'l-Bahá finds no corroboration in his writings or in other pilgrim's notes. It is true that certain dedicated Bahá'í martyrs, caught up in spiritual ecstasy, are reported to have felt no pain under torture. However, to establish this as a teaching of 'Abdu'l-Bahá is perhaps an overstatement. — ED.

other messengers, who will come, in the future as in the past, when the world requires them. If men's minds are fixed on miracles, which prove nothing except themselves, they will be less open to the reception of truth, or be closed entirely to the Divine Message.

He says, also, that if miracles are ascribed to the founders of a religion and become engrafted upon it, they will inevitably be simulated by priesthoods and other pretenders to Divine authority to mislead, delude, and defraud the ignorant masses of mankind, as illustrated by the greater part of the past history of Christianity, and by the hundreds of quacks and impostors who at the present day practice their shameful impositions upon the people in the name of Christ.

So, too, 'Abbás Effendi discourages everything tending to center attention upon himself or to exalt his personality into an object of devotion or worship. He has had numerous applications for his photograph, but always declines to have it taken.* His reply to these requests is: "I do not wish to have men think of my personality or my form. The personality changes, the form passes away: there is nothing permanent about them. All this must die—must pass out of the recollection of men. But deeds and words never die. These are my sign: it is these only which I wish to leave to the believers and to the world."

His only claim or description of himself is, "Servant

*Photographs of 'Abdu'l-Bahá were rarely taken before his visit to America in 1911–1912.—ED.

‘ABDU’L-BAHÁ
at the gate of his house.

'ABDU'L-BAHÁ
walking near the gate of his house.

of God," or "Servant of Bahá'u'lláh," or "Servant of the servants of Bahá'u'lláh."

Bahá'u'lláh bestowed many titles upon him (see pp. 103–104), but as to these he says that they were all given by favor, and that they mean but one thing—"Servant."

As might be expected from this lack of self-assertion, 'Abbás Effendi's life is spent in quiet and unassuming work. His general order for the day is prayers and tea at sunrise, and dictating letters or "Tablets," receiving visitors, and giving alms to the poor until dinner in the middle of the day. After this meal he takes a half-hour's siesta, spends the afternoon in making visits to the sick and others whom he has occasion to see about the city, and the evening in talking to the believers or in expounding, to any who wish to hear him, the Qur'án, on which, even among Muslims, he is reputed to be one of the highest authorities, learned men of that faith frequently coming from great distances to consult him with regard to its interpretation.

He then returns to his house and works until about one o'clock over his correspondence. This is enormous, and would more than occupy his entire time, did he read and reply to all his letters personally. As he finds it impossible to do this, but is nevertheless determined that they shall all receive careful and impartial attention, he has recourse to the assistance of his daughter Rúḥá, upon whose intelligence and conscientious devotion to the task he can rely. During the day she reads and makes digests of letters received, which she submits to him at night.

In his attention to these various duties he is absolutely unremitting. The month which I passed in 'Akká was the Muhammadan fast of Ramadán, which, as all other Muhammadan observances, was scrupulously kept by 'Abbás Effendi and his followers, for the sake of peace and to avoid the imputation of social innovation. This fast requires abstinence from food between sunrise and sunset. The effect of this privation upon him, in addition to that of his assiduous activity, was very marked, and towards the end of the fast he frequently appeared to be in a state of great exhaustion.

I have adverted to his frugal and abstemious habits in matters relating to his personal comfort. Several incidents further illustrating this trait were told to me. On one occasion he was going to Haifa, and asked for a seat in the stage. "Your Excellency," said the driver, "surely wishes a private carriage." "No," replied 'Abbás Effendi. The driver thought this parsimony in a man of his position. At Haifa, while he was still in the stage, a fisherwoman came to him in great distress, saying that all day she had caught nothing, and must go home to a hungry family. He gave her five francs, and turning to the stage-driver said: "You now see the reason why I would not take a private carriage. Why should I ride in luxury when so many are starving?"

The Master's habit of wearing cheap clothes troubles his family. I was told of a conspiracy a few months before to impose a cloak of better quality upon him without his knowledge. His wife procured the necessary money from her brother, who is in the habit of acting as banker for the family, and furnished a tailor with the required cloth, who proceeded to make the garment. They knew very well that the Master would not wear expensive clothes if he knew it, but, counting upon his inattention to such matters, hoped that he would not notice the quality.

But unfortunately the tailor bungled the cloak. It did not fit, had to be returned several times; and in the goings to and fro which ensued, its cost came to 'Abbás Effendi's knowledge. Thereupon he sent for his brother-in-law and said to him: "You must sell that cloak and charge me with whatever loss there may be upon it: such an amount of money will buy four cloaks, one of which is good enough for me; the others can be given away."

His daughter Rúḥá relates that when her sister was recently married she had no trousseau, and for the ceremony merely donned a clean dress. People asked her father why he had not given his daughter bridal garments. He replied, "My daughter is warmly clad and has all that she needs for her comfort. The poor have not. What my daughter does not need I will give to the poor rather than to her."

Early during my stay in 'Akká the following curious incident was related to me. The Master happened to have a fine cloak of Persian wool which had been given to him. When a poor man applied to him for a garment, he sent for this cloak and gave it to the applicant. The

'ABDU'L-BAHÁ IN HIS GARDEN

man took it and demurred, saying that it was only of cotton. "No," said 'Abbás Effendi, "it is of wool"; and to prove it he lighted a match and burnt a little of the nap. The man still grumbled that it was not good. 'Abbás Effendi reproved him for criticizing a gift and appeared not a little vexed at his ungrateful conduct. But he terminated the interview in this extraordinary fashion—by directing an attendant to give the man a *mejidi* (a coin worth about four francs). "If any one vexes him," continued my interlocutor, "he always gives him a present."

I was at a loss to understand this singular procedure at the time; but an incident which occurred later during my stay threw light upon it. One day the Master was distributing coats to poor men, in accordance with his custom, to which I have referred above (p. 4). In this distribution he carefully selected the donees, judging from his personal knowledge in each case whether the charity was merited, and making a record of those to whom coats were given. On this occasion there was one man who was very insistent in his demand for a coat, but whose application 'Abbás Effendi for some reason did not approve. The man continued to persist, and the Master to refuse, finally repulsing the beggar with a good deal of acerbity. After some time, however, what did he do but bring this same man into the large court where the coats were hung upon a line, and give him the choice of the lot! The man tried on three, and, finding one which suited him, took it away.

Madam Canavarro saw the incident and afterwards asked 'Abbás Effendi to explain it. He smiled and said: "Did you notice that?"—and then, calling her attention to the backs of his hands, which had been somewhat scratched and torn in managing the crowd, he continued: "My body is still under the law. You see how these people may injure it. It is necessary that I should control them—that I should put them down. But, having put them down, I must show them that I did not do it in unkindness. And so, too, if I find it necessary to display some temper, I must take care that my actions show my motive, in order that my example may not be misunderstood."

The Master has, as may be inferred from what I have already said, a very tender, sensitive, and sympathetic nature. To his appreciation of the suffering and discontent which it causes among women I chiefly attribute his dislike to the institution of polygamy, remarkable in one who has been all his life surrounded by those who practice it. This is shown not only by his persistent refusal to adopt it for himself, notwithstanding the very powerful influences (see above, p. 120) which have urged him to do so, but by the reticence which he habitually maintains when the subject is introduced. It is evidently a matter upon which, because of his surroundings, he does not wish to express himself with freedom.

Many things suggestive of his sympathy and tender-heartedness were told to me. I have referred to his habit of eating very simply and but once a day. This is not his invariable custom, since, when he has guests, he entertains them generously, in fact exquisitely, and eats with them. His family say, however, that he always prefers a simple repast; and if it happens that he has just come from visiting the poor, elaborately prepared food is especially distasteful to him.

Busy as he is, it would much relieve him to delegate distributing alms to some of his followers. This, in fact, he sometimes does, but rarely, for this reason. On these occasions the poor frequently resort to artifices, as by going away after receiving money and returning to secure double or triple alms. These artifices are likely to be met, by any one except himself, with impatience or harshness, and this the Master does not like. To the poor and ignorant above all, he says, we should always be kind.

Once he was entertaining a wealthy lady who had her maid with her. The latter stood behind her mistress' chair at dinner. 'Abbás Effendi was uneasy. At length he called for a chair, placed it beside him, and asked the maid to be seated. Then he addressed his conversation to her, telling her, among other things, to be content; that those who served were often more loved by God than those whom they served.

I was told of the case of a consumptive who had been almost deserted by his friends, as frequently happens in 'Akká, Syrians having a superstitious fear of the disease. The mother and sisters of this young man hardly entered his room. His food was brought in by a

'ABDU'L-BAHÁ
walking, with believers behind.

servant, and he was left to reach it and otherwise to care for himself as best he could.

The house in which he lived was near that occupied by the Master, and the ladies of the latter's family saw this sad sight from their windows. No woman, of course, could offer assistance under the circumstances; but the Master heard of it from them, and thereafter went daily to the sick man, took him delicacies, read and discoursed to him, and was alone with him when he died.

In his dealings with men and in the relief of suffering, differences of religious opinion have no weight with the Master. Men of all faiths are absolutely the same to him. He commonly associates a Muslim and a Christian with him in regulating his charities. I usually noticed one or both of these faiths represented among those who were assisting him in the distribution of alms or clothing. The ideal of human life which he strives, first of all, to promote, is fraternal cooperation among all men.

During the fast of Ramadan considerable discomfort is caused among the poorer Muhammadans by the fact that, when exhausted by the long fast of the day (from sunrise to sunset), they have not the means to provide a sufficiently substantial meal to restore their strength. It was the Master's habit, while I was in 'Akká, to provide every second day a supper at sunset for many such persons.

A year or two ago a wealthy American lady, a friend

of 'Abbás Effendi, spent some months in Haifa. On going away she asked permission to make him the donation of a sum of money, for his own use or for that of the Cause. He replied that he could not himself accept a gift from her; but that if she wished to do something for him, she should educate the two little girls of a Christian schoolmaster in Haifa, who had recently lost his wife, was very poor, and in much trouble. She accordingly sent these children to a school in Beirut.

There are in 'Akká about ninety Bahá'ís of whom I think I have met all the men. The restrictions imposed by Muhammadan social customs, which, as I have said, the Bahá'ís here observe for the sake of peace and harmony, prevented me from meeting the women. These Bahá'ís are all Persians, living in 'Akká in voluntary exile in order to be near their "Master." The fact that, also for the sake of peace, they are not permitted by him to make propaganda within the dominions of the sultan explains, no doubt, the absence of other nationalities among them.* The attractions of their native country do not weigh as a straw against the privilege of living near 'Abbás Effendi; and nothing except his wish, which is absolute law to his followers, could induce them to leave him. This touching and eloquent tribute to the character of 'Abbás Effendi is only an expression of the fundamental characteristic of all Bahá'ís whom I

---

*Bahá'u'lláh Himself commanded His followers not to make converts in the Holy Land. This restriction was observed by 'Abdu'l-Bahá and Shoghi Effendi and continues to be observed today. — ED.

A GROUP OF BAHÁ'Í MEN
Taken in 'Akká, circa 1909.

'ABDU'L-BAHÁ WITH FRIENDS
Taken in Haifa, February 1919.

have known—that is, the absolute devotion of themselves, their possessions, and their lives to the cause of
their faith and its representative. I am told that it is the
dearest wish of the millions of Bahá'ís in Persia[51] to
make the pilgrimage to 'Akká, and that, if such a thing
were possible, they would migrate there *en masse* for
permanent residence. But at present even pilgrimage is,
except in rare instances, forbidden by 'Abbás Effendi.
In the earlier years of Bahá'u'lláh's imprisonment there,
when access to him, or even entrance into the city, was
impossible for Bahá'ís from Persia, the pilgrimage was
frequently made for the mere purpose of seeing him at
the window of his room in the prison, from a point
without the walls of 'Akká.

I have never known a community which seemed to
enjoy such a general distribution of the sterling
qualities and virtues of character. They are industrious
and self-controlled; in appearance they are cleanly and
thrifty. Their faces are all sincere, honest, kindly, in-
telligent, and generally strong. Their school is attended
by about twenty bright-looking boys (girls are excluded
by Muhammadan custom), who are, among other
things, industriously studying the English language, and
have made considerable progress in acquiring it.

In their intercourse with each other, and, so far as I
have had the opportunity to observe, with others, the
Bahá'ís continually overflow with kindliness and good-
will. They seem like a single family whose members
bear the liveliest affection for one another. I can even

easily credit the statement made to me that when the persecutions were at their height in Persia, it happened more than once that a Bahá'í, having been arrested by mistake in place of another who had been denounced, permitted the error to go undiscovered, and suffered execution rather than endanger his fellow-believer.

To a Bahá'í there is no recommendation of character and trustworthiness equal to that of being a Bahá'í. This confidence in the character of Bahá'ís extends also, as I have learned from conversation with other citizens of 'Akká, to those who are not of their faith. I am told that they are frequently chosen as fiduciaries and trustees by Muslims and Christians.

One observes among them a feeling of fellowship and complete equality as men, regardless of the distinctions of wealth and poverty or high and low degree. I saw this feeling expressed many times; as when, during the exposition of the doctrines by some teacher in my room, the boy who served my meals would enter without remark and respectfully take a seat before him.

There is also among them an atmosphere of intense religious conviction and spiritual life, — yet quite without apparent emotion or excitement, — which forcibly impresses one who is accustomed to the torpidity prevailing in Western lands in regard to those things. Professor Browne remarks (*A Traveller's Narrative,* introduction, p. xxxix.):

> The spirit which pervades the Bábís [Bahá'ís] is such that it can hardly fail to affect most powerfully all subjected to its in-

'ABDU'L-BAHÁ DESCENDING MT. CARMEL
with a group of pilgrims.

fluence. . . . Let those who have not seen disbelieve me if they will; but, should that spirit once reveal itself to them, they will experience an emotion they are not likely to forget.

Nothing could be more true. In the presence of a number of them, aglow, as they all are, with the fire of love, conviction, and determination, one feels—however he may believe, he feels—that scepticism about the reality of spiritual existence is a trifle absurd, and that things unseen must be as certain as things seen.

If we analyze this peculiar spirit of the Bahá'ís; if we seek to penetrate that which marks them off from other men, the conclusion to which we are brought is that its essence is expressed in the one word *Love*. These men are Lovers; lovers of God, of their Master and Teacher, of each other, and of all mankind. This is the name which they are fondest of applying to themselves, and it is that which most intimately indicates their distinctive characteristics. Their love goes out in all these directions with the fervor of the lover's passion, but a passion free from all gross elements. It is this which has sustained them in their sufferings and martyrdoms, and now inspires their eager devotion to their cause. To some this fact will have an immense possible significance; for they will remember that seers have said that there is a Divine Love of which the ordinary human passion is but the darkened and corrupted shadow, and which, searching, strenuous, and pure, it is sometimes given to men to feel.

REFERENCES

1. An overstatement, of course. Bahá'u'lláh's family had at one time been extremely wealthy, but his father, Mírzá Burzurg-i Núrí, lost much of his money and influence during Bahá'u'lláh's lifetime. See *Bahá'u'lláh: The King of Glory*, pp. 15–18.

2. Násiru'd-Dín Sháh was attacked by three young Bábís on August 15, 1852. The attempted assassination was the result of the conspiracy of a small number of Bábís residing in Tehran. Their leader, Mullá Shaykh 'Alí Turshízí, 'Azím, eventually made a full confession which cleared Bahá'u'lláh of any connection with the crime. See *The Dawn-Breakers*, pp. 599–600, 636–37; *God Passes By*, pp. 62–64, 104; *Bahá'u'lláh: The King of Glory*, pp. 74–76.

3. On another occasion, the Greatest Holy Leaf recalled this incident vividly in these words: "Suddenly and hurriedly a servant came rushing in great distress to my mother. 'The master, the master, he is arrested—I have seen him! He has walked many miles! Oh, they have beaten him! They say he has suffered the torture of the bastinado! His feet are bleeding! He has no shoes on! His turban has gone! His clothes are torn! There are

chains upon his neck!' My poor mother's face grew whiter and whiter." (*The Chosen Highway*, pp. 40–41)

4. There were also other factors which led to the release of Bahá'u'lláh from prison, including the intervention of the Russian ambassador, Prince Dolgorouki. See *God Passes By*, p. 104, 106.

5. Bahá'u'lláh set out from Tehran on January 12, 1853, and arrived in Baghdad on April 8, 1853. He was escorted by a member of the imperial body-guard and an official of the Russian legation to Iran. Besides his immediate family—his wife, Navváb, and children, 'Abdu'l-Bahá and the Greatest Holy Leaf—his brother, Mírzá Músá (Áqáy-i Kalím) and half brother Mírzá Muḥammad-Qulí, with their families, accompanied him into exile. See *The Dawn-Breakers*, p. 650; *God Passes By*, pp. 106, 108; *Bahá'u'lláh: The King of Glory*, p. 102.

6. Other accounts provide a slightly different version of Bahá'u'lláh's withdrawal to Sulaymáníyyih, in Kurdistan. Shoghi Effendi states: "Suddenly, and without informing any one even among the members of His own family, . . . He departed, accompanied by an attendant, a Muḥammadan named Abu'l-Qásim-i-Hamadání. . . . Shortly after, that servant was attacked by thieves and killed, and Bahá'u'lláh was left entirely alone . . . " (*God Passes By*, p. 120).

See also, the account of the Greatest Holy Leaf in *The Chosen Highway*, pp. 50–51; 'Abdu'l-Bahá's account in *A Traveller's Narrative*, pp. 64–65; and, *Bahá'u'lláh: The King of Glory*, pp. 115–22.

7. During the Baghdad period, there were three governors of the city; none of them were relatives of Bahá'u'lláh or his enemies. See *God Passes By*, pp. 131, 142, 149–50; *Bahá'u'lláh: The King of Glory*, pp. 480, 482–83.

The archenemies of Bahá'u'lláh in Baghdad were Mírzá Buzurg Khán-i Qazvíní, the Persian consul, and Shaykh 'Abdu'l-Husayn-i Tihrání, the personal representative of the shah. See *God Passes By*, pp. 145–46; *Bahá'u'lláh: The King of Glory*, pp. 135–54 passim.

8. The summons was couched in courteous language and requested that Bahá'u'lláh visit the Government House. Bahá'u'lláh arranged to meet the officials in the mosque opposite that place. See *My Memories*, pp. 20–21; *God Passes By*, pp. 147–48; and *Bahá'u'lláh: The King of Glory*, pp. 154–55.

9. According to Balyuzi, the meeting began late in the day. (*Bahá'u'lláh: The King of Glory*, p. 155)

10. Shoghi Effendi states: "Of the exact circumstances attending that epoch-making Declaration we, alas, are but scantily informed. The words Bahá'u'lláh actually uttered on that occasion, the manner of His Declaration, the reaction it produced, its impact on Mírzá Yahyá, the identity of those who were privileged to hear Him, are shrouded in an obscurity which future historians will find difficult to penetrate." (*God Passes By*, p. 153)

See also, *My Memories*, p. 22; *Revelation I*, pp. 278–80.

11. Bahá'u'lláh left Baghdad for Istanbul with His fam-

ily, His brothers Mírzá Músá and Mírzá Muḥammad-Qulí, and some twenty-six disciples. See *My Memories*, pp. 25–26; *Materials*, pp. 16–17; *God Passes By*, pp. 155--56; *Bahá'u'lláh: The King of Glory*, pp. 156–58, 175–77.

Of Bahá'u'lláh's departure, Shoghi Effendi writes: "A caravan, consisting of fifty mules, a mounted guard of ten soldiers with their officer, and seven pairs of howdahs, each pair surmounted by four parasols, was formed . . . At times on horseback, at times resting in the howdah reserved for His use, and which was often-times surrounded by His companions, most of whom were on foot, He, by virture of the written order of Námiq Pá<u>sh</u>á, was accorded, as He traveled northward, in the path of spring, an enthusiastic reception . . . " (*God Passes By*, p. 156)

12. Bahá'u'lláh and His companions were not prisoners in Istanbul, but were free to come and go. In all probability, however, the women were confined to the house by Islamic custom. Cf. *My Memories*, pp. 37–39; *Bahá'u'lláh: The King of Glory*, pp. 197–216 passim.

13. The exiles had arrived in Istanbul on August 16, 1863. They remained there for less than four months, departing on December 1, 1863. Cf. *God Passes By*, pp. 158–161; *Bahá'u'lláh: The King of Glory*, pp. 204–206.

14. The journey to Edirne actually lasted twelve days. See *God Passes By*, p. 161; *Bahá'u'lláh: The King of Glory*, p. 204.

15. Bahá'u'lláh and His family were first lodged in a two-story caravansari known as <u>Kh</u>án-i 'Arab. Three

days later, they moved to a house in the Murádíyyih quarter of the city. See *My Memories*, pp. 42–43; *Materials*, p. 19: *God Passes By*, pp. 161–62; *Bahá'u'lláh: The King of Glory*, pp. 218–21.

16. This house is known as *Bayt-i Amru'lláh*, the House of God's Command or the House of the Cause of God. See *My Memories*, p. 43; *Materials*, p. 19; *God Passes By*, p. 162; *Bahá'u'lláh: The King of Glory*, p. 221.

17. See reference 10, above.

18. Mírzá Yaḥyá was regarded by most Bábís at this time as the titular head of the community. Cf. *God Passes By*, pp. 28–29. For a fuller discussion of Mírzá Yaḥyá's claims from a Bahá'í point of view, see *E. G. Browne and the Bahá'í Faith*, pp. 33–41.

19. A slightly different version of these events has been recorded by Ustád Muḥammad-'Alíy-i Salmání, the bath attendant, in his memoirs. See *My Memories*, pp. 50–53.

20. There appear to have been a number of attempts to poison Bahá'u'lláh in Edirne. Shoghi Effendi mentions that the well of Bahá'u'lláh's house was poisoned by Mírzá Yaḥyá. (*God Passes By*, p. 166) He further relates that Bahá'u'lláh's serious illness was caused by poison smeared on his teacup by this same person. (Ibid., p. 165) The teacup story is also related by Mírzá Muḥammad-Javád-i Qazvíní in his historical epitome. (*Materials*, pp. 22–23)

The Greatest Holy Leaf's version of the cause of Bahá'u'lláh's illness (that the rice had been poisoned) is repeated in her published interview with Lady Blomfield. (*The Chosen Highway*, p. 60) Browne had heard this story independently. (*A Traveller's Narrative*, p. 359) As Phelps notes in his footnote (pp. 60–61), this version of the story was reversed by the Azalís who made the preposterous claim that Bahá'u'lláh had accidentally poisoned himself while trying to poison Mírzá Yaḥyá.

21. Cf. *God Passes By*, p. 166.

22. Shoghi Effendi describes Azal's response to the Súriy-i Amr as follows: "Mírzá Yaḥyá's request for a one day respite, during which he could meditate his answer, was granted. The only reply, however, that was forthcoming was a counter-declaration, specifying the hour and the minute in which he had been made the recipient of an independent Revelation, necessitating the unqualified submission to him of the peoples of the earth in both the East and the West." (*God Passes By*, pp. 166–67)

23. Bahá'u'lláh's withdrawal lasted two months, not four months. See *My Memories*, p. 99; *God Passes By*, p. 167.

24. The causes of Bahá'u'lláh's banishment from Edirne were complicated. See *God Passes By*, pp. 178–79; *Bahá'u'lláh: The King of Glory*, pp. 250–54.

25. Cf. *Materials*, pp. 28–29; *God Passes By*, p. 180; *Bahá'u'lláh: The King of Glory*, pp. 258–59.

26. Mírzá Muḥammad Javád-i Qazvíní records that Bahá'u'lláh left Edirne "accompanied by his sons . . . , his family and his disciples, sixty-eight souls in all."

(*Materials*, p. 29) However, these were joined upon their arrival in Gallipoli by several companions who had been arrested in Istanbul. In her interview with Lady Blomfield, the Greatest Holy Leaf fixes the number of persons who embarked from Gallipoli for 'Akká at seventy-two. (*The Chosen Highway*, p. 63) But, of course, Mírzá Yahyá and some of his followers, along with four Bahá'ís, were eventually separated from the other exiles and sent to Cyprus. Shoghi Effendi numbers those banished to 'Akká at "about seventy." (*God Passes By*, p. 181)

The journey from Edirne to Gallipoli, in carts and wagons, lasted about four days. See *Materials*, p. 29; *The Chosen Highway*, p. 62; *God Passes By*, p. 180; *Bahá'u'lláh: The King of Glory*, p. 260.

27. In her published interview with Lady Blomfield, the Greatest Holy Leaf states that the exiles remained in Gallipoli for a week. (*The Chosen Highway*, p. 62) Mírzá Muḥammad Javád-i Qazvíní indicates that they were there for ten days, arriving on August 9, and embarking for 'Akká on August 19, 1868. (*Materials*, pp. 29 and 31) Áqá Riḍáy-i Qannád remembered the period as "a few days." (*Bahá'u'lláh: The King of Glory*, p. 261) Shoghi Effendi says "three nights." (*God Passes By*, p. 181)

28. Shoghi Effendi states: "The government's original order was to banish Bahá'u'lláh, Áqáy-i-Kalím and Mírzá Muḥammad-Qulí, with a servant to 'Akká, while the rest were to proceed to Constantinople. This order, which provoked scenes of indescribable distress, was,

however, at the insistence of Bahá'u'lláh, and by the instrumentality of 'Umar Effendi, a major appointed to accompany the exiles, revoked." (*God Passes By*, p. 181)

29. The European consuls had visited Bahá'u'lláh before his departure from Edirne, not at Gallipoli. (See *Materials*, p. 27; *Bábí and Bahá'í Religions*, pp. 191–200; *God Passes By*, p. 180; *Bahá'u'lláh: The King of Glory*, pp. 256–58, 456–59)

30. At least one of the prisoners, Áqá Muḥammad Ibráhím-i Náẓir, left the ship under guard to make purchases. Nabíl-i A'zam, who was at the time imprisoned in Alexandria, has recorded that it was through sighting Áqá Muḥammad-Ibráhím in the street that he came to know of Bahá'u'lláh's presence in the city. See *Bahá'u'lláh: The King of Glory*, pp. 265–68.

31. Áqá 'Abdu'l-Ghaffár's attempted suicide took place while the ship was at port in Haifa. He was one of the four Bahá'ís who was forced to accompany Mírzá Yaḥyá to Cyprus. He sought to end his life rather than be separated from Bahá'u'lláh. Nonetheless, he was rescued and sent on to Cyprus. See *Materials*, p. 44: *God Passes By*, p. 182; *Bahá'u'lláh: The King of Glory*, p. 269.

The Greatest Holy Leaf, in her published interview with Lady Blomfield, recalled: "The friends, though prostrated by sickness, worn out by the wretchedness of the voyage, and crushed by this repeated blow, determined to refuse submission. One friend, in his dire distress, jumped into the sea, but was saved.

"Bahá'u'lláh and the Master cheered us. 'Why did you

jump into the sea? Did you wish to give a banquet to the fishes?' asked Bahá'u'lláh." (*The Chosen Highway*, p. 65)

32. Of the landing in Haifa, the Greatest Holy Leaf recalled, in another interview: "At length we arrived at Haifa, where we had to be carried ashore in chairs. Here we remained for a few hours. Now we embarked again for the last bit of our sea journey. The heat of that month of July was overpowering. We were put into a sailing boat. There being no wind, and no shelter from the burning rays of the sun, we spent eight hours of positive misery, and at last we had reached 'Akká, the end of our journey." (*The Chosen Highway*, p. 66)

The exiles arrived in Haifa shortly after sunrise on August 31, 1868, and embarked for 'Akká a few hours later. See *Materials*, p. 44; *God Passes By*, p. 182; *Bahá-'u'lláh: The King of Glory*, p. 269.

33. Shoghi Effendi writes: "All fell sick, except two, shortly after their arrival. Malaria, dysentery, combined with the sultry heat, added to their miseries." (*God Passes By*, p. 187)

34. Actually, only three of the exiles died at this time, although one, Mírzá Áqáy-i Kashání (Jináb-i Munír), had died earlier on the journey to 'Akká. See *Materials*, p. 46; *Bahá'u'lláh: The King of Glory*, p. 283; *God Passes By*, p. 187.

35. Balyuzi provides a list of sixty-seven companions who entered the prison of 'Akká with Bahá'u'lláh. Two more friends joined these prisoners a few days later. (*Bahá'u'lláh: The King of Glory*, pp. 276–77)

36. In another published interview, the Greatest Holy Leaf recalled: "So closely were we watched that we had been in 'Akká six or seven months without being able to get into touch with Mírzá 'Abdu'l-Ahad, a devoted Bábí disciple, who had been sent by 'Abdu'l-Bahá to 'Akká some time before our arrival, and had opened a shop." (*The Chosen Highway*, p. 67)

37. Concerning the death of the Purest Branch, see also *Materials*, pp. 49–50; *God Passes By*, pp. 188–89; *Bahá'u'lláh: The King of Glory*, pp. 311–14.

38. In her interview with Lady Blomfield, the Greatest Holy Leaf explained: "Meanwhile the war between Russia and Turkey was in progress. More barrack room was required for the soldiers. Bahá'u'lláh protested against the friends being crowded in with the soldiers. By that time the Governor had become friendly and consented to allow the family to leave the fortress, and live in a little house which a Christian merchant had let to us.

"How we rejoiced in our liberty, restricted though it was. Only three times had we been permitted to go out, for even an hour, from the prison barracks during the whole of that first two years.

"How tired we were of those three little rooms!" (*The Chosen Highway*, p. 68)

Bahá'u'lláh and his family were kept in various houses in 'Akká for a period of months before finally being moved to the house of 'Udí Khammár. See *Materials*, p. 50; *God Passes By*, p. 189; *Bahá'u'lláh: The King of Glory*, p. 315.

39. According to Balyuzi, two of the Azalís—Sayyid

Muḥammad-i Iṣfahání and Áqá Ján-i Kaj-Kuláh—were housed, upon their arrival in 'Akká, over the city gate. From this vantage point they kept watch and reported to the authorities anyone whom they recognized as a Bahá'í trying to enter the city. (*Bahá'u'lláh: The King of Glory*, p. 317)

40. There were actually seven Bahá'í conspirators. See *Materials*, pp. 52–55; *God Passes By*, p. 189; *Bahá'u'lláh: The King of Glory*, p. 325.

41. Actually, three partisans of Azal were killed: Sayyid Muḥammad-i Iṣfahání, Áqá Ján-i Kaj-Kuláh, and Mírzá Riḍa-Qulíy-i Tafrishí. The latter had been a Bahá'í, but was expelled by Bahá'u'lláh. He joined the ranks of the Azalís. See *Materials*, p. 55; *God Passes By*, p. 189; *Bahá'u'lláh: The King of Glory*, p. 320 and 325.

42. The woman, Badrí-Ján, was removed to Cyprus against her will. (*Bahá'u'lláh: The King of Glory*, pp. 336–37) The identity of the "surviving Azali" mentioned here is not clear.

43. For 'Abdu'l-Bahá's description of Bahá'u'lláh's move from 'Akká, see "Prison Gates Open," *Bahá'u'lláh and the New Era*, pp. 34–38.

44. For another version of this story, see *Bahá'u'lláh: The King of Glory*, pp. 342–44.

45. The details of this story are related somehat differently in *Episodes*, pp. 13–14 and in *The Dawn-Breakers*, pp. 208–209.

46. For Munírih Khánum's own account of her first marriage, see *Episodes*, pp. 18–19.

47. According to Munírih Khánum, she lived in the

house of Mírzá Músá (Áqáy-i Kalím) in 'Akká for about five or six months. (*Episodes*, p. 29; *The Chosen Highway*, p. 87)

48. The Bahá'í marriage ceremony consists of the exchange of a marriage vow, accompanied by such prayers and readings as the couple may choose.

49. Concerning Munírih Khánum's life and marriage to 'Abdu'l-Bahá, see also *Episodes*, 20–31; *The Chosen Highway*, pp. 84–90; *Bahá'u'lláh and the New Era*, pp. 53–55; *Bahá'u'lláh: The King of Glory*, pp. 339–48.

A letter written on behalf of Shoghi Effendi to the National Spiritual Assembly of the Bahá'ís of the United States and Canada reads: "With regard to Munírih Khánum's account of her life, concerning which certain questions have been raised by one of the believers; what has been written by Munírih Khánum herself in that account, and also the references to the subject made by Nabíl in his Narrative should be taken as the accurate standard and not what has been reported in Dr. Esslemont's book." (*Bahá'í News*, No. 133 [February 1940] p. 2)

50. Cf. *The Chosen Highway*, p. 90.

51. A more accurate estimate of the number of Bahá'ís in Iran at this time (1902) is one or two hundred thousand. See Peter Smith, "A Note on Babi and Baha'i Numbers in Iran," *Iranian Studies*, vol. 17 (Spring-Summer 1984) no. 2–3, p. 297.

BIBLIOGRAPHY

'Abdu'l-Bahá. *Memorials of the Faithful*. Trans. and annotated by Marzieh Gail. Wilmette, Ill.: Bahá'í Publishing Trust, 1971.

['Abdu'l-Bahá]. *A Traveller's Narrative Written to Illustrate the Episode of the Báb*. Trans. by Edward G. Browne. Cambridge University Press, 1891 (Amsterdam: Philo Press, 1975).

Bahá'u'lláh. *Epistle to the Son of the Wolf*. Trans. by Shoghi Effendi. Wilmette, Ill.: Bahá'í Publishing Trust, rev. ed., 1976.

Balyuzi, H. M. *'Abdu'l-Bahá: The Centre of the Covenant of Bahá'u'lláh*. London: George Ronald, 1971.

———. *The Báb: The Herald of the Day of Days*. Oxford: George Ronald, 1975.

———. *Bahá'u'lláh: The King of Glory*. Oxford: George Ronald, 1980.

———. *Edward Granville Browne and the Bahá'í Faith*. Oxford: George Ronald, 1975.

Blomfield, Lady (Sitárih <u>Kh</u>ánum). *The Chosen Highway*. London: Bahá'í Publishing Trust, 1940 (Wilmette, Ill.: Bahá'í Publishing Trust, 1956).

Browne, E. G., comp. *Materials for the Study of the Bábí Religion*. Cambridge University Press, 1918 (1961).

Cole, Juan R. and Momen, Moojan, eds. *Studies in Bábí and Bahá'í History, Volume Two: From Iran East and West*. Los Angeles: Kalimát Press, 1984.

Esslemont, J. E. *Bahá'u'lláh and the New Era: An Introduction to the Bahá'í Faith*. Wilmette, Ill.: Bahá'í Pulishing Trust, 4th rev. ed., 1980.

Gail, Marzieh. *Bahá'í Glossary*. Wilmette, Ill.: Bahá'í Publishing Trust, 1955.

Ḥaydar-'Alí, Ḥájí Mírzá. *Stories from the Delight of Hearts: The Memoirs of Ḥájí Mírzá Ḥaydar-'Alí*. Trans. and. abridged by A. Q. Faizi. Los Angeles: Kalimát Press, 1980.

Honnold, Annamarie, comp. *Vignettes from the Life of 'Abdu'l-Bahá*. Oxford: George Ronald, 1982.

Ḥuseyn of Hamadán, Mírzá. *The New History of Mírzá 'Alí Muḥammad, the Báb*. Trans. by Edward G. Browne. Cambridge University Press, 1893 (Amsterdam: Philo Press, 1975).

Momen, Moojan. *The Bábí and Bahá'í Religions, 1844–1944: Some Contemporary Western Accounts*. Oxford: George Ronald, 1981.

———, ed. *Studies in Bábí and Bahá'í History, Volume One*. Los Angeles: Kalimát Press, 1982.

Moneereh Khanum (Munírih K͟hánum). *Episodes in the Life of Moneereh Khanum*. Trans. by Mirza Ahmad Sohrab. Los Angeles: Persian American Publishing Company, 1924. (Los Angeles: Kalimát Press, 1986)

Muḥammad-'Alíy-i Salmání, Ustád. *My Memories of Bahá'u'lláh.* Trans. by Marzieh Gail. Los Angeles: Kalimát Press, 1982.

Nabíl-i A'ẓam (Muḥammad-i Zarandí). *The Dawn-Breakers. Nabíl's Narrative of the Early Days of the Bahá'í Revelation.* Trans. and edited by Shoghi Effendi. Wilmette, Ill.: Bahá'í Publishing Trust, 1932.

Phelps, Myron H. *Life and Teachings of Abbas Effendi.* New York: G. P. Putnam's Sons, 1903 (2nd rev. ed., 1912).

Ruhe, David S. *Door of Hope: A Century of the Bahá'í Faith in the Holy Land.* Oxford: George Ronald, 1983.

Shoghi Effendi. *God Passes By.* Wilmette, Ill.: Bahá'í Publishing Trust, 1944.

A Synopsis and Codification of the Kitáb-i-Aqdas, the Most Holy Book of Bahá'u'lláh. Haifa: Bahá'í World Centre, 1973.

Taherzadeh, Adib. *The Revelation of Bahá'u'lláh.* Volumes 1–3. Oxford: George Ronald, 1974–1983.

Thompson, Juliet. *The Diary of Juliet Thompson.* Los Angeles: Kalimát Press, 1983.